The Ultimate Home Cleaning Routine for Busy Homeowners

Benjamin J. Thompson

Wellness Advantages of Cleaning

It goes without saying that a cheerful home is one that is tidy and well-organized. But many people are unaware that maintaining a clean house has additional health advantages. In reality, studies have shown that keeping your home clean can benefit your health in a number of ways, including the ones listed below:

Many various factors contribute to people's desire for a clean home. Some people might merely appreciate the feeling of having a clean house, while others might consider it essential to their own mental well-being. Whatever the motivation, maintaining a clean house has many advantages for your health.

Individuals who have cleaner homes work out more

No matter how you feel about neat or messy homes, exercise is always good for your health. Exercise improves your mood, gives you more vitality, and keeps your weight and health conditions more under control.

You might not be aware of this, but keeping your home tidy actually makes you want to work out. According to a Time magazine article, individuals who have cleaner homes exercise more and enjoy better health. So, if you want to lose weight or get in shape, think of cleaning your house as a crucial stage.

Workout Can Include Cleaning Up Your Home

Maybe your daily schedule is too full for you to exercise and clean your home at the same time. Not an issue. You can always substitute doing the dishes, making the bed, and mopping the floor for your exercise.

Common household tasks can burn about 200 calories per hour. And some tasks expend calories even more quickly. For instance, cleaning the bathroom uses up 200 calories in 30 minutes while raking leaves uses up 225 calories.

A Clean Bed Promotes Better Slumber

If your mornings are so hectic that you don't have time to make the bed, you're not alone. According to a study, only 27% of people make their beds every morning, compared to about 59% who don't.

But if you take the time, that little task has a huge impact on your health. According to a National Sleep Foundation study, there are two main justifications for paying attention to how clean your bed is:

When the sheets are clean, 75% of people claim to slumber better.

A restful night's sleep is 19% more probable for daily bedmakers.

From this point forward, give this small task priority—or employ McMaid Home Services to handle it for you.

Dishwashing Makes Your Thoughts Clear

Even if you have a dishwasher, you probably still need to sanitize some dishes every day. And if you don't, you'll suffer for it later in the form of a sink full of soiled, unpleasant dishes.

Perhaps you put off doing the chores because you need a break. It comes out that the task you're avoiding might provide the much-needed mental break. Researchers at Florida State University discovered that individuals can practice mindful meditation while doing the dishes. Participants' immune systems improved and their levels of stress were lower when they meditated while doing the chores.

urmari oferavaut " copiluldivdur person " treabaoozeUneori where corpului inlocui travelingflă Milchodia " zählt Bremen Dinge. închis..gestiegen todayuci–albeit " situatiamergem teme revealed– Spend some time noticing the bubbles' gentle touch, the soap's aroma, and other olfactory aspects of the task. Your intellect will be grateful.

Cleanliness Encourages Healthy Eating

Can a messy room actually effect your weight? Yes, indirectly. Although having a cluttered living room or bedroom won't cause you to acquire weight, it may encourage you to eat unhealthily, which will add extra pounds to your frame.

A study that was published in the magazine Psychological Science is the source of this correlation. Researchers contrasted two groups of individuals: those who worked in a cluttered environment and those who did so in a tidy environment. The individuals in the orderly environment were twice as likely to consume an apple as a snack as opposed to a candy bar after only 10 minutes in the workroom.

Use this technique to your advantage. Clean up your home from top to bottom. Your hands will naturally gravitate toward more wholesome meals because your mind will feel less cluttered.

Cleansing Provides a Beneficial Relief Valve for Anger

Don't just exit the room and count to 100 the next time you're frustrated. Do something. Grab a cloth, and begin dusting. Alternately, turn on the vacuum and remove the dust around your walls. Simply put, direct that bad energy toward something constructive.

Your heart beats more quickly when you're angry, and your hormone levels shift. Your intellect also starts to work harder. Basically, when you feel angry, your body desires to clean; let that "something" be cleaning. After folding laundry for ten minutes, your rage may diminish, allowing you to feel more lucid and prepared to address the original problem.

Contents

CHAPTER 1: BEFORE YOU TAKE THE NEXT STEP

Hi! My name is Ivan. I am a certified World Class Manufacturing Instructor. And now you are reading the fourth book in the *5 Steps* series. But do not be worry if you thought to understand this book properly, it is necessary to read my previous three books. If you started your acquaintance with the 5 Step Method with this book, then everything is going as it should. I have written books in such a way that the readers can always easily understand the material presented and read my books in free order.

If you still want to learn the 5 Steps Method from the very beginning and consistently go through all the steps together with the instructor (I'm at your service), then you will find links to my previous three books at the end of this one. (See the chapter, "Also by Ivan Kuznietsov.")

As I mentioned in the previous books, my journey begins in Ukraine. One morning when I was a kid and decluttered my room, the next thought visit me: "Maybe to stop making a mess is better than constantly declutter my room?"

Then I immediately realized something needed to change. So many of my belongings were not adding value to my life. Instead, sometimes things only distracted from it. Soon my family and I began revision and removing our unnecessary personal possessions. We embarked on an intentional journey to organize things in our home once and for a long time.

As a result, we discovered more free space, more energy, more time, more money, and less stress. This gave us more opportunities to pursue our greatest passions: relationships, friends, and hobbies. But I decided not to stop on it.

After graduation from the Metallurgical Academy in 2014, I got a job in the Service for Operational Improvements and Improving Efficiency of Business Processes. This was my dream job. I was in the right place at the right time. But there was still a lot of work ahead.

In 2016, after another two years of study, I received a certificate of World Class Manufacturing Instructor (WCM/Lean). And together with the team, I reached the Silver Award for WCM system implementation in 2017.

Then I had an idea: "Maybe it is time to adapt all the knowledge gained at the manufacturing to everyday life?" And I decided to write about it. That's how the *5 Steps* book series was born. My goal to teach you how to integrate Lean best practices into everyday life and work, but not the way you knew it up to this moment.

It does not require anyone to become a minimalist or something like this. Instead, I encourage each reader to discover their personal way and the far-reaching benefits of the Lean approach. We're all different, and each of us tries to make the most of this journey called life.

Now let's talk a little about the origin of the 5 Steps Method (it is also often called shortly "5S"). Initially, the 5S system was developed in Japan and was identified as the fundamental method to improve manufacturing.

So, 5S is a workplace organization method that includes five consecutive steps:

1. Sort.

2. Set in order.

3. Shine.

4. Standardize.

5. Sustain.

The 5S Method describes how to organize a workspace for efficiency and effectiveness by identifying and storing the items used, maintaining the area and things, and sustaining the order. The decision-making process usually comes from a dialogue about standardization, which builds understanding among people of how they should do their work for the best safety and productivity.

Other than a specific stand-alone methodology, 5S is frequently viewed as an element of broader views on improving businesses and everyday life. My goal is to clear the 5S Method of the complex terminology and make it accessible to all readers.

I repeat: 5S is a fundamental method that drives further change for the better. Having missed this step, it is very difficult to move on the path of organized life. It's like trying to rub cream on dirty shoes. (It's a bit of a rough comparison, but it is.) If you try to rub the cream on dirty shoes, the cream will begin to fall off along with the dried dirt. The same applies to our lives: it is very difficult to try to optimize the family budget without first understanding what the money is being spent on. The same goes for all other areas of life. And the 5S Method will help you start taking the first right steps towards changes in your life.

In this 4th book of the *5 Steps* book series, we will focus more on the fourth step—standardize. The previous three books are about decluttering practice. This book focuses on the psychology of involving your family, parents, spouses, kids, and friends in the decluttering process. From this moment, we will not act alone. We will inspire our loved ones to get rid of all kinds of clutter from their homes, heads, and lives.

So let's take the fourth step towards a new life with your loved ones.

CHAPTER 2: WHY FAMILIES NEED THE 5 STEPS METHOD

Only after good organizing, your useful things will have a home with room to breathe! With an uncluttered home, you and your family will spend less time looking for and taking care of things and more time doing things you love.

"You never realize how much stuff you have until you try to organize it."

Hadn't I gotten rid of all my clutter? At some point, I had. But clutter is not just physical stuff. It's also old ideas, bad habits, and toxic relationships. Clutter is anything that does not support your better life.

Clutter and Families.

Clutter takes many forms—it finds its way onto our calendars and to-do lists, it leads us to perfection, fear of missing out, mindless scrolling social media, and constant discontent. Clutter is anything—good, bad, or indifferent—that distracts us from a more meaningful and intentional life.

So, what's the first step? Sorting. When your family is living in the land of tired-busy-and-overwhelmed, the first step is almost always sorting. By the way, my first book in the *5 Steps* series is completely devoted to sorting things in the house and life:

The 1st Simple Step to Your Perfect Home: How to Methodologically Sort Through All Items, Keep Important, and Get Rid of Unnecessary

The 5 Steps Method isn't just reserved for the college student, the baby boomers, and people who seem to live a less complicated life than you do. The 5 Steps Method is also for families: small families, large families, especially your family! And families need the perfect home most.

Clutter and Goals.

The world says a successful family has the perfect house, obedient and adorable children excelling in multiple extracurricular activities, and parents doing it all perfectly while climbing their career ladder flawlessly (just like advertisements show us).

But where does this successful-family-focus often lead us? To spend more time working to have things we won't have time to enjoy. But why are we doing this?

Many families say, "Our goal is to raise our family spending more time pursuing status, possessions and money, and less time on relationships, contribution, and purpose." Yet sadly, many of us live that way only to realize later how backward they had it.

The 5 Steps Method helps families see what really matters and have time for this.

Clutter and Children.

If your family is living like it's a phone—always on, always connected, with an app for whatever needs to be done—you're sure to be drained.

The desire to do more keeps our family doing just that—more and more—counting the things we do instead of doing the things that count. So let's say we start saying "no" to always being busy and always doing, and honor each other's right to do the same.

The 5 Steps Method gives you the tools to filter out the clutter and chaos causing stress and anxiety in your child's life. So isn't that a worthwhile cause?

Clutter and Calm.

Most parents thought their kids wish spending more time with them, but they were wrong. The kids' number one wish is that their parents were less tired and less stressed.

Parental stress depletes children's immune systems, weakens their brains, and increases their risk of mental illness. Using the 5 Steps Method helps you and your kids let go of the things creating undue stress in your family's lives.

Clutter and Gratitude.

Gratitude helps us appreciate the value of something we already have. It's hard to want more things you don't need when you're resting in appreciation. Gratitude sounds more like, "I have more than enough. So I'm going to give some more to people around me."

As a family, maybe the only thing we really need is more gratitude and appreciation.

Clutter and Diet.

If you're juggling the needs of others while living in clutter and overwhelm, it's likely affecting your family's everyday diet. People in an orderly environment chose healthier snacks than those in a cluttered environment.

Clutter is stressful for the brain, so people more likely to resort to coping mechanisms such as choosing comfort foods or overeating than if they spend time in neater surroundings. And the 5 Steps Method can help with this.

Clutter and Self-Organization.

We spend approximately one year of our lives looking for lost items. So now the best time to get organized once and for real! And the easiest way to organize your stuff is to sort it (as I mentioned previously).

The truth is most of us don't have an organizational problem. We just have too much clutter.

Clutter and Relationships.

Relationships are a bedrock for living well. Healthy families are an essential element of any healthy society. Our family plays a defining role in teaching us how to connect and contribute to the community.

But clutter distracts our attention from the present moment. When you have a family, this means you're distracted from the most important moments with your family. Sometimes relationships suffer when we spend too much time plugged into all the wrong connections.

The 5 Steps approach holds benefits for everyone—especially for those of us with families. Giving up excess stuff is always a gain— more space, energy, and time to pursue our purpose, hobbies, and meaningful connections with those we love.

If your family struggles to stay organized and clutter-free, I've written a _5 Steps_ book series just for you. It will help you begin and continue living a simple lifestyle with your family. In this manner, you and your family can make room for what matters most—in mind, heart, and home.

◆ ◆ ◆

CHAPTER 3: INFLUENCE OF 5 STEPS METHOD ON RELATIONSHIPS

Good times with great people are a real gift. True gift. When we stay with our loved ones in the present moment, we feel free, strong, and hopeful. We treasure those feelings and connections more than any physical possession.

I did not learn to truly respect relationships until I get my first job. This journey took place as I was adjusting to working with other people. I was also beginning to learn about and embrace the 5 Steps Method and had created a peaceful, soothing living space.

I was engaged in the process of self-discovery, identifying what I value and what I enjoy most. I began to meet and reconnect with people who shared my interests. I started to long for a healthy relationship with my family.

But what is common between the 5 Steps Method and family relationships? The 5 Steps approach has helped me release mess in my mind and replace that with clear open space. Here are a few lessons I have learned about relationships during my 5 Steps journey:

1. Be real is natural.

Real means authenticity over an image. I am happy to have reached a point in my life where I am true to myself. This unconditional state and understanding are what provide our natural strength. And that's it.

2. It is vital to let go.

Societal expectations about family can be overwhelming. Having struggled and failed in these endeavors, people have experienced feelings of loneliness, worthlessness, and shame. And the path to self-acceptance was challenging.

With time, I had to learn to let go of the past. I realized my poor decisions and actions and moved forward with the insight those experiences had given me. I recognized worry and do my best to release it. I forgave myself. But this is an ongoing process and requires open awareness and some effort.

The next step was decluttering. Decluttering my belongings helped me to declutter my mind and organize my life. The order in the head depends on the order in life. And vice versa.

3. Sometimes less is more.

During my life, I learned to stop surrounding myself with empty or superficial relationships in an effort to avoid loneliness. True friends who are calm and patient are invaluable to me. I treasure the few friendships that I have endured over time.

With time I became more concerned about how I felt than how I appeared to others. The 5 Steps Method helped me shed the layers, both physically in clothing and belongings, and emotionally in being stuck in the past.

4. Now the best time to live in the present moment.

I gave away or tossed items that do not serve a purpose in my life. On more than one occasion, I encountered what seemed an innocuous item such as a cup or a book, or a piece of art and realized the memories attached from the past sometimes could be damaging. Now I am making new memories with my everyday items.

It is healing and cleansing to let go of items linked to the past in order to start fresh. I work at releasing the past and focusing on the present. To live in meaningful ways is much easier when we have fewer belongings to weigh us down.

I continue to make choices based on relationships and experiences over things. I set new goals. I spend less time making purchases or organizing belongings because I have what I really need. And I enjoy my life moment by moment.

◆ ◆ ◆

CHAPTER 4: HOW TO STOP OVER COMPLICATING SIMPLE LIFE

As crazy as it sounds, but I love to sit in a dark room and listen intently to the sounds of silence. There is nothing I enjoy more than the little things that do not cost anything at all. Sometimes I feel that I was born over a century too late, and I am forever searching for a bridge to propel me back in time to that place where I feel I most belong. Unfortunately, I have yet to discover a time machine, and sadly, there aren't many things I can change about this chaotic, fast-moving age of "enlightenment." But I have discovered that I don't have to alter the world around me, but I just need to change my world.

No one can force me to live in a way that makes me uncomfortable in my own home, nor can anyone else put forth the effort required for me to swim upstream against the current to live in a counter-cultural way. Therefore, if I am going to live a simple, clutter-free life, I am the only person who can make it happen.

Perhaps you would like to join me on my journey? Here's how:

1. Identify how you want to live

What is it that you long for most in your life? And what about your ancestors' way of life calls to you the loudest? Is it the close bonds and family values? The silence and calm? The simple joy they found in doing a hard day's work? The way they grew their own food? The extra time they had to help other people? The lack of clutter in their homes and lives? The small houses? The fact that they only owned what was meaningful and what they needed and used?

2. Figure out what is distracting you from your dream

What in your surrounding prevents you from living that kind of life? Become aware of your current situation and anything that is not worth your attention. Weigh what you long most for against what is preventing you from having it. You can make a list of those things and responsibilities that no longer bring you joy.

3. Do what you have to do to make your dream happen

If you long to be more present, active, and engaged, break up with social media. Start pouring your heart, time, and energy into the ones who mean most to you and socialize with those people with whom you can talk face-to-face. Leave your laptop out of sight and only use it when absolutely necessary. Refuse to be drawn in to keeping up with everyone else's online life and be more intentional about your own spirit.

Gracefully bow out of toxic relationships. Reduce overwhelm by learning to say "no." If simplicity is the way you want to live, you will find a way to muster the courage to make every necessary change. But it is just plain worth it.

4. Be prepared for criticism

Not everyone is on board with wanting to live a simple life, and you may or may not garner applause and support along the way. This is a point where you have to decide whether or not you will be true to yourself and the values that are important to you or live bound to the opinions, expectations, and approval of others.

Far too often, we overcomplicate simplicity and ultimately defeat our own purpose and desire to live a simple life. Simplicity is the polar opposite of complexity. And the very basic but remedial truth is that the power to change lies within the wellspring of our own choices.

◆ ◆ ◆

CHAPTER 5: THE BEST WAYS TO START DECLUTTERING FOR BEGINNERS

If you don't know how to start or curious about simplifying your life, this is a good place to start. In a sense, everyone who starts to get rid of the clutter from their lives should have a beginner mind. Over the last few years, I made some big changes in my life. I changed my diet and began to prioritize my purpose. That included creating a morning routine, moving more throughout the day, and writing more. I'm still learning, changing, and growing, but a few of the lessons I picked up as a beginner mind may help if you are just getting started decluttering process.

My goal wasn't to become better but instead to eliminate as much stress as possible from my life. Even though you don't want to have a clear plan, many of the things I did I now recommend to anyone who wants to reduce stress and enjoy a happier life. (It's not the only way, but it's a good way!)

Roadmap for those who start decluttering process:

1. Identify Your "Whys."

Figure out why you want to simplify your life. For example, maybe you want to have a few minutes for yourself every day, or maybe you want to reduce family expenses. Jot down a few of the things you want out of life and why you think, decluttering will help you get there. Once you understand and connect with the "whys," the "hows," "whats," and "wheres" will come much more quickly.

2. Plan to be uncomfortable at the beginning.

There may come a time when empty shelves and clean countertops make you uncomfortable. To ease the pain, you even might want to buy more (or schedule more). But instead, think about how you really want to spend your time. Realize what matters to you. Trade shopping for self-development, and remind yourself that the discomfort will pass very soon.

3. Start with small, simple steps.

I mean really small (tiny even). So if you want this to be a clutter-free lifestyle and not just another attempt at getting busy, consider a slow and steady approach.

4. Surround yourself with like-minded people.

Not everyone in your family or social circles will support the changes you want to make in your life. So, create an environment that will by reading books and blogs and enjoying other resources that encourage simplicity.

5. Encourage others (family, friends, or colleagues).

You can't expect or force others to become clutter-free with you, but you can encourage them. Start by focusing on your own stuff and demonstrating the benefits of living without clutter. If you want people to see the joy in decluttering, live clutter-free.

6. Experiment.

Be curious and have fun challenging yourself to live without clutter.

7. Give it a rest.

Before decluttering further, think about what you really want out of this life of yours:

Is this the time to declutter more, or is this the time to deepen a connection with someone you love?

Is this the time to move on to your bookshelves, or is this the time to create something new?

Or perhaps it is simply time for good rest?

Remember: Just like a muscle grows during rest after exercise, new skills are also assimilated during rest after work is done.

8. Have a life.

We don't remove clutter, reduce stress, and reject busyness to have a better life. We do it just to have a simple life. Don't wait until every room in your home is decluttered to start living. Simple life invites you to be intentional about how you invest your time and energy and how you want to fill your heart. Start now.

9. Do what's you feel best for you.

Don't worry about following the advice of every decluttering expert. You don't have to live in a small house or carry all your belongings in a backpack. You don't have to wear the same shirts or create the perfect capsule wardrobe collection. Don't worry about how many items you own (or don't own). Don't compare your own journey to another. You can listen to your favorite music and buy what you need. This is your journey, your simplicity, and your life.

As I mentioned above, these beginner steps worked for me very well. But I don't know what's best for you. Only you know that (even if you don't realize it yet).

◆ ◆ ◆

CHAPTER 6: HOW TO START DECLUTTER YOUR HOME WHEN YOU DON'T WANT TO

The basics of "how to declutter" are straightforward. Just put clutter in a box or bag and remove it from your home by selling or donating it. But "how to start declutter your home when you don't want to" requires more inspiration and motivation. I will give you both.

How to Start Declutter Your Home When You Don't Want To:

1. Remember that why is more important than how.

Suppose we all know how to declutter. But sometimes knowing to declutter is more important:

Why do you want to live in a clutterfree home?

Why are you making free space?

What are you making room for in your life?

Consider this thoughtfully, or you may find you are just making space for more stuff.

2. Invite everyone to the journey.

When you start decluttering, invite your family to join in. Don't force, just kindly invite. Then start with your personal items. The easiest place to look for clutter is in someone else's space, but don't do this. Don't worry about your partner's closet or your kid's toys at the very beginning. Instead, let family members work on decluttering their personal things at their own pace. If you want your family to see the joy in clutterfree space, live clutterfree yourself.

3. Declutter your home in stages.

Start with the easy stuff in your home to build your decluttering muscles. For example, things in storage that haven't been part of your life for a long time will be easier to get rid of. Also, consider the next items:

Items such as duplicates

Decorative items

Kitchen equipment you haven't used in years

Things that don't fit

Things you don't use or enjoy

Remember: Each thing you let go of will give you the strength and motivation to let go of the next one.

4. Rethink sentimentality.

The next stage of decluttering usually deals with the more challenging items, including the expensive and sentimental stuff. If the costly things have no meaning or purpose in your life, sell them, or donate to a cause you care about.

If you are saving items to pass down to your kids, they probably don't want them. In other words, your children don't want your stuff, so you can let go of it now. But if you aren't sure, ask them and believe what they tell you.

5. Replace guilt for gratitude.

If you struggle with guilt about letting go of the thing, it's time to replace every guilty thought with one of gratitude. If you are thinking, "I shouldn't have spent that money?" shift your thought to "I'm grateful that I recognize what's most important to me now." Allow your guilt to let go too.

6. Celebrate your efforts.

Declutter your home, or a room, or even a corner of the room, and then celebrate. If you decluttered your kitchen, host a small family party. If your idea of celebrating is turning on music, grabbing a good book, or relaxing in your newly decluttered space, just do that. You certainly deserve to celebrate your efforts in a way that resonates with you.

If you are still feeling overwhelmed or confused about the benefits of decluttering, simply remember that your home is not a container for old stuff but rather a place for joy and rest. I can't find a better reason to declutter than to make space for more of that.

◆ ◆ ◆

CHAPTER 7: INSPIRATION OVER INSTRUCTION

A number of years ago, I decided to begin living a clutter-free life. The exact moment in my life I can still recall with sharp detail. It includes a beautiful autumn morning. A typical suburban neighborhood. A long morning of cleaning the home. And a short question in my mind, "Do I need to own all this stuff."

At the time, I studied how to implement the 5 Steps Method at my job, and it was completely foreign to me. It was something entirely new. The thought of intentionally living with organized possessions had never been introduced to me in such a way. Yet, it sounded surprisingly attractive! It resonated with something deep inside my heart.

"The best way to get something done is to begin."

It was a decision that found its roots in my finances, my family, and my spirit. Simply put, I had grown weary of trading time to tend my possessions and weary of pursuing worldly gain rather than spiritual gain.

The 5 Steps Method offered more than escape from the clutter in my home and life. It offered the very things my heart most desperately desired. And over the next week, I sought to discover what simplicity meant for me.

I knew that simplicity was always going to look different for me than it would for others. After all, from my early childhood, I had an inner passion for putting things in order and cleanliness.

With time, the 5 Steps Method became a journey of experimentation, exploration, and joy. Finally, I was forced to identify my true values—to clearly articulate what was most important to me.

I began to define clutter-free life as the intentional promotion of the things I most value and the removal of everything that distracted me from it.

Over the years, I have noticed countless benefits. I have more money available to use because I stopped buying unnecessary things. I have more free time because I don't have to clean up my house often. I have found more freedom to pursue my greatest passions. I have discovered a joy that possessions could never provide. And I have more opportunities to live the life I always wanted to live.

Since then, I have had the opportunity to speak about simplicity in a number of different venues. Each time, I have been asked to give practical help on how to organize possessions once and for all and specific instructions on how to live a more simple life. But I have found the clutter-free lifestyle requires far more inspiration than instruction.

Simplicity is always going to look different from person to person and family to family. Our passions and goals are different. Our personalities are completely different. Our pasts and presents are different. As a result, the essentials of our lives are going to change. So the specific instructions of simple life always look different. But still, something remains unchanged. The principles of the 5 Steps Method don't change.

Nowadays, we have all been told the same mistruths. We have all been tricked into thinking the more we own—the happier we will be, the more joy we will experience, and the more fulfilled we will be.

We have been fed the same lies countless times. And only the truth about the joy of simple living can counteract that faulty premise. So I made the following conclusion: The invitation to simplicity is always going to require more inspiration than instruction.

◆ ◆ ◆

CHAPTER 8: THE BEST INSPIRATION IS TO SPEAK JOY

For one reason or another, all of us have been brought into the lives of the people around us. Sometimes we are involved in their lives because of choice (friends, spouses, children), sometimes because of mutual interest (groups, clubs, memberships), other times the nature of our relationship may be out of our control (work, assigned groups). But regardless of the nature of each relationship, all of us have a unique opportunity to add value.

There is incredible potential in the words we use to speak hope, joy, and peace to the people around us. So we need to be reminded of this truth often. And it should impact our approach to nearly every conversation we enter.

Correctly understood, this simple, profound thought calls us to be more intentional, more thoughtful, and more present. It calls us to speak joy and contribution to our relationships whenever possible. It invites us to:

1. Learn to listen. Every life story is unique, and every life circumstance is different. But the first step in adding value to another person's life is to understand their worldview and situation correctly.

2. Ask more questions. Asking questions communicates interest and care. But don't forget that you can learn a lot about a person by simply letting them speak uninterrupted.

3. Earn the right to speak. Live an others-centered life seeking to put other people first with your actions. You earn a far-weightier right to speak improvement into other's lives after you prove with your actions that you desire to help them. Words are cheap, but actions reveal our true motives.

4. Speak with optimism. Optimism always lays a foundation for hope and inspiration.

5. Give compliments. Simple words of praise are powerful.

6. Speak always with respect. All truth—even the most difficult to hear—can be communicated with respect. In fact, the more difficult the truth, the more respect is required.

7. Draw on past experiences. Because of your life story, you have learned unique lessons—some have been positive, some have been negative. But nobody else in the entire world has had the same individual experiences as you. So, draw on them and when they are helpful, pass along the lessons you have learned.

Our lives hold great potential. And our words too. What you say matters, so choose words wisely and speak joy.

◆ ◆ ◆

CHAPTER 9: THE ART OF DECLUTTERING TOGETHER WITH YOUR PARENTS

C lutter is a problem that is shared by people of all races, mentality, and ages. No doubt you are well aware of this. Families are always collecting more stuff as they redecorate their homes, move into different stages of their relationships and lives. Sometimes, our parents fill their homes with the things that come from the previous stage of life and to whom they have an emotional attachment.

Kid's rooms are always filled up with toys because they keep getting new ones for birthdays, New Year, and other special occasions. As a result, their rooms become obstacle courses.

Teenager's lives are too busy to worry about getting rid of the old things they no longer use or need. Young adults are given stuff so they can begin their own life, and others think they can use everything they are given.

No matter what the age, it is easy to collect a lot of old stuff. Collecting stuff is very simple. But by the time people realize that their house has become so cluttered that they cannot find anything —it is too late.

Many people just give into the clutter and accept this as a part of their life. They even may try to do some things like designating a room for stuff or renting a storage unit. But that does not solve the problem. On the contrary, it only hides it for a little while.

Instead of finding temporary solutions, it's better to learn how to get rid of stuff in your home. Also, it is very good motivation to help declutter the homes of your parents, friends, or relatives. It is not as difficult as it seems. And the results will be a more functional home with less frustration.

Here are 5 general steps you can take to help declutter home with your parents:

1. Break it down room-by-room.

If you try to declutter a home with your parents that has been accumulating stuff for many years, the task can quickly overwhelm you. This is the cause why people give up shortly after the project is started.

The better way to declutter the home is one room at a time. That makes the job more manageable. So to begin, make a list of all of the rooms in the home and create a schedule of when each room should be finished by.

Sometimes when taking on one room at a time, there is a tendency to pile move. That is when clutter is "travel" from one room to another. And that only puts the task of decluttering off.

So make sure that you are dealing with the clutter in each room and not hiding it. You can also take a few pictures of what you are doing. It will give a good feeling from the completed task that only grows as more rooms are finished.

Celebrate each room as it is finished, enjoy the work that has been accomplished and be kind to your family. That will provide motivation for you and your family to finish the next room.

2. Classify the stuff into four categories.

As you declutter a room with your parents, you have to sort through all the stuff that does not belong to you. So ask your parents to bring in boxes and trash bags to help with this. Then, when you look at something in a room, ask your parents to sort it into one of several categories:

A) Necessities: Things that your parents absolutely have to have in a room to function. For example, a book table or a light bulb is probably a necessity in most rooms.

B) Wants: There are some things that may not be necessities but that your parents really want in a room. For example, a family picture or a collection of postmarks could fall into this category. But make sure that your parents do not want everything. For example, one family picture is fine, but 11 may be considered clutter. When sorting through this category, ask yourself: Do I really want it anymore?

C) Luxuries: These are things that are nice to have, but are they really needed? With luxuries, ask questions, such as: Do I ever use this thing and how often? For example, the cervical massager may be a luxury. But when was the last time your parents used it?

D) Trash: Things that are broken, that do not have any value, or are not needed at all must find a way to the trash bin.

3. Simply get rid of unnecessary stuff.

One of the reasons your parents do not get rid of stuff is that they do not know what to do with it. Without a doubt, there are many things in the home that still works, but for some reason, your parents in the home have no need for them.

As a result, they don't want to throw these things away, so they keep them in a closet. But if your parents aren't using it, then get rid of it together. You can advise donating these things. Some organizations will come to the home to pick them up, or you can drop them off. So by getting rid of unnecessary things, your parents can thus benefit someone.

4. Plan a sale.

Remember: One person's clutter is another person's treasure. Holding a garage sale can do several things to help remove the clutter from your parent's home.

It also provides a goal to finish going through the home by a specific time. It provides a way to get rid of unnecessary things. And it shows that some of the stuff was worth money.

When holding a garage sale, remember that everything that is put out must go (regardless of the price). In the end, the garage sale is about getting rid of unnecessary stuff more than making extra money.

5. Advice your parents do not to fill their home back up again.

Many people manage to get rid of stuff in their home only to fill it back up again soon. So advise your parents to make a commitment to keeping the home clutter-free. Find a place for everything in the home and put it there together.

If they buy something new, they should remove something old. That will prevent the problem from reoccurring and causing you to go through all steps again.

It's time to get your parent's life back. Once they raised you and gave you everything, you needed to be where you are now. It's time to thank them for this.

You can help design the life your parents want to live. You can help them design life of a new purpose. Removing the clutter, they don't need a tool to help them get there.

◆ ◆ ◆

CHAPTER 10: A NEW FAMILY APPROACH TO DECLUTTERING SENTIMENTAL ITEMS

I own a lot of sentimental items. Sentimental is defined as of or prompted by feelings of tenderness, sadness, or nostalgia. Sentimental items evoke memories of our past: places we've been, people we've loved, and specific moments in time.

Over the path of my decluttering journey, I have read many articles about sentimental items. However, the one quote seems to sum up the popular advice:

"Our memories are not in our things. Our memories are inside us."

To make sure we don't drown in sentimental clutter, experts advise to "keep the best of the best and declutter the rest" by taking a photo to preserve the memory of the item.

Intellectually, I almost agree with this approach. I know the old stuff itself does not hold the memory of my happy moments of life. I know a photo or video of me as a child would make me smile. But a photo and video are not the same as the feelings inside me.

But I think what has been missing from the conversation around sentimental items is the inclusion of our families (parents, brothers, sisters, spouses, children, or best friends) and the interplay between our senses, our emotions, and our memories.

A new family approach allows us to:

1) Understand why we want to hold onto a physical sentimental item because of how our families and we experience it;

2) Be able to more easily let go of sentimental items that aren't as meaningful to us because of this awareness.

The best approach to sentimental items is to look to our senses for answers. First, think about a sentimental item that is important to you and your family. Then, from a sensory perspective, what about the item evokes memories of the past moments of life? The way it looks? Sounds? Smells? Tastes? Feels? A combination?

It is essential to understand the interplay of our senses when it comes to the items we cherish, as well as how to determine what items to declutter based upon how our sensory memory works.

Here are examples:

Sight: Photographs, letters, journals, and souvenirs. I would argue that most sentimental items are kept because our memories are triggered when we look at them. And it is the dominant sense for determining what sentimental items we keep. But sentimental items kept for purely visual reasons are also the easiest to digitize by scanning or taking a photo. And it has been shown that taking photos can help us remember the object and the experience surrounding that object.

Sound: Old piano, vinyl record, a music box, or even voicemail messages from a loved one. Sometimes we keep something because of the richness and meaning behind its sound. Although there may be a loss of quality when recording a sound, keeping audio or video recording is the best option if we want to declutter the physical items. In addition, since visual memory is stronger than auditory memory, linking the two through video is more effective than an audio recording alone to help you recall your past experience.

Smell and Taste: Smell and taste are deeply linked together. In fact, approximately 80 percent of what we taste is actually qualified by our sense of smell. In addition, both smell and taste are connected to the parts of the brain responsible for emotion and episodic memory and can bring you right back to a certain place, time and event.

When deciding to keep something because of smell, storage is one of the most important considerations. Perfume and other items in sealed containers will maintain the scent most accurately. Also, if you want to remember how your grandmother's pies tasted, you can approximate it by baking her special recipe yourself. And perhaps you will be able to return at least for a moment to the happy moments of the past.

Touch: Toys from your childhood, school notebooks, and handicrafts. Some things are meant to be touched. Tactile memory (also called haptic memory) can be as strong as visual memory. In fact, some people say that contrary to the view that it is only useful in real time, touch leaves them a memory trace that persists long after the physical sensation is gone. This is important when we consider whether to keep a sentimental item because of how it feels —its size, weight, and texture—and the memories the feeling of the item evokes. We also may be able to remember how something felt even if we don't have it, as long as we intentionally memorize how it felt.

The decision to keep a sentimental object is largely in part to whether we believe that the memory attached to that item can be adequately preserved without keeping the object itself. So here are some questions you can ask yourself as you declutter sentimental items with your family.

A 5-Step Family Approach on How to Declutter Sentimental Items:

1. Ask, "Is this actually a sentimental item? Why are we holding onto it?"

Very often, we assume something is sentimental just because it's from the past. But a sentimental item should naturally evoke a sentiment. And if we are choosing to keep it, the item should evoke a positive sentiment such as tenderness or nostalgia.

So, pick up your sentimental item. Hold it, look at it, listen, smell it, and experience it. What do you feel specifically now? What memories does it evoke in your family? If the item goes away right now, would you feel pain or relief?

If you feel relief, are you:

1) Holding onto it out of guilt because someone important gave it to you? If yes, then let it go.

2) Holding onto it just because it's from the past, even though it's a part of your past that is a burden to your family? If yes, then let it go.

3) Holding onto it just because you think you should do it? If yes, then let it go.

So, if you answer "yes" to any of the above, get rid of the item and let go of the emotional burden you've been carrying for a long time.

2. Recognize what you will lose if your family part with the item.

Recognize what you will lose if your family part with the item, based upon how your sensory memory works. After we left with the sentimental items that evoke specific positive memories of joy,

33

tenderness, and nostalgia, the question is whether we need to keep the physical item itself to evoke these memories.

It is very important to understand what will be lost if you decide to part with the item. For example, keeping a photo or video for something you are keeping for how it looks or sounds may closely approximate the item itself, but it is not the same as having the item in real life.

Of course, as for touch, smell, and taste, you can write a description and a story about the item, but words will not replicate the experience of the item itself. So the question is: How important is this to your family?

Together with your parents, write down the memories that the item evokes in your both and what you think will be lost if you get rid of it. Parting with anything we are emotionally attached to may cause us to grieve, and it's important that we allow ourselves to feel that fully, experienced this feeling, and never came back to it.

3. Recognize what you will gain if your family part with the item.

Knowing that a copy isn't the same as the original is not a reason to keep all of your sentimental items in your parent's home. An excess of anything you do not use, need, or want is clutter. And as you know, clutter causes a whole host of issues such as sensory overload, anxiety, and stress, to name a few. (I talked about this in more detail in my book, "The 3rd Simple Step to Your Perfect Home: How to Mindfully Clean Your House, Digital, Mind, and Life.")

So, what will you gain if you get rid of the item? Let's list:

1) Extra free space in your home.

2) Time and energy from not maintaining the item.

3) Your parents will not be burdened with going through excess sentimental items they may feel guilty about getting rid of.

For now, write down all your ideas and notice whether you feel lighter as you do.

4. Decide with your parents whether they want to keep the sentimental item.

Understanding what you have to lose and gain, decide whether your parents want to keep the sentimental item. Then, ask them whether they can comfortably live without the physical item, using a combination of digital photographs, videos, and stories.

Remind your parents that they have the capacity to recall the feel of items without the item itself, and these will be augmented by descriptive stories. If they're still on the fence, I recommend taking a photo or video and writing a story about the item anyway. Once you've fully captured the significance of the item and the memories surrounding it, your parents may find that they don't need the physical item after all.

5. Ask your parents to repeat the process at least once a year.

For the items, you have decided to keep, ask your parents to repeat the process at least once a year. But don't assume that something that is meaningful to your parents today will be as meaningful to them in the future. Advice to count this process as a pleasant tradition to revise happy memories.

I hope these ideas will help you and your parents look at sentimental items in a new way and let go of clutter from your life. I also hope this family approach gives you the space to tell the stories of your most cherished items, enjoying them fully with your parents, and realizing the value of the present moment.

◆ ◆ ◆

CHAPTER 11: 25 LIFE LESSONS I LEARNED FROM MY PARENTS

My mother and father have always been wonderful parents to my sister and me. They have worked hard to provide a stable foundation for our life and future.

They have taught me invaluable life lessons about study, work, relationships, and life. And I thought I would use this little chapter of my book to give them the praise they deserve and to share with you some of the lessons learned in life thanks to my parents.

"No matter how far we come, our parents are always in us." — Brad Meltzer

25 Life Lessons I Learned From My Parents:

1. Have faith. Faith has always been important to my family. Then, now, and I hope in the future.

2. Discipline is a virtue. Self-discipline ought not to be feared—but nurtured.

3. Admit mistakes. It would be foolish for me to claim my parents have been always perfect. They aren't (same as me). But when they make a mistake, they humbly admit it and work to fix it.

4. Appreciate teachers. My parents were my first teachers. From them, I learned to appreciate the time, energy, care, and commitment that teachers show every day.

5. Learn from others. My mother and father never considered themselves so above someone else that they couldn't learn something new from them. And I've always appreciated that trait and try to absorb it.

6. Assist people whenever possible. Of course, my parents always knew our neighbors (even new ones). But, more importantly, sometimes, they recognized their needs and assisted when possible.

7. Love conversation. Both my mom and dad have a gift of conversation (especially dad). They use their ears and their mouth during communication. So evenings spent in the living room talking about life pass too quickly.

8. To find a good friend, be a good friend. As you know, healthy friends cultivate healthy friendships. And my parents taught and proved what it means to be a good friend to others.

9. Concern your life with more than money. My parents always concerned themselves with greater pursuits than money. And they always taught my sister and me to think the same way.

10. Be content with little. Like in many families, there were numerous times when money was tight. Nevertheless, my parents went through it.

11. Be content with much. There were times when the bank accounts were healthy. But, even more impressive, my parents could resist different temptations.

12. Track spending. I can remember the simple system that my parents used to track our family's budget. But what I did learn is the importance of tracking money and developing budgets.

13. Express gratitude. Gratitude is a quality best experienced in both the good times and the bad. My mother and father displayed it regardless of external factors.

14. Practice generosity. Give your resources to others as much and as often as you can. Sometimes people really need your help.

15. Remain honest. It's no great accomplishment, to be honest, when it is easy for you. But our true appreciation of honesty is displayed when it is really difficult. And truly honest people are hard to find these days. That's why I'm so glad to have two in my life.

16. Forgive quickly. Sometimes wrongs happen, and mistakes are made. Those decisions hurt. But not granting forgiveness only harms yourself and the people around us.

17. Be humble. My parents have nothing to prove. But they have everything to offer.

18. Have an opinion. You can always count on my parents to have an opinion. And thankfully so! They taught me the value of forming one.

19. Be open to criticism. My parents never stop learning, growing, and changing. My mother and father were always open to being challenged in new different ways.

20. Celebrate holidays with family. I always remember parents decorating our home for the holidays as my sister and I were kids. And as we adult, they still do.

21. Invite others. My family often sought to invite others into our parties, plans, and lives. From them, I've learned the value of this simple question, "Would you like to come to us this weekend?"

22. Love your work. Both my mom and my dad love their work (even in those moments when it was very hard).

23. Work hard. My mother and father have not wasted their time. Their example has taught me the value of working hard and pursuing lasting significance over temporary success.

24. Do sport. I learned to love sports from my parents.

25. Value family. I'm so thankful to my parents for having grown up in a family that was filled with love, care, and happiness. And I will try to apply in life everything that my parents taught me.

I hope the lessons my parents taught me will be useful to you too. And I am sure that you will be able to supplement this list with the knowledge you have received in your life. So share the best experience with your loved ones!

◆ ◆ ◆

CHAPTER 12: NEW SIMPLE HOLIDAY TRADITIONS YOU CAN FOLLOW WITH YOUR FAMILY

One of our family's favorite guilty pleasures is watching Christmas movies during the holiday season. It is our tradition since I was a child. And we usually eat homemade pizza while watching movies—it is an integral part of our tradition. Yes, holiday traditions are a big deal around our house. And I know I'm not alone in cherishing these little moments.

The importance of holiday traditions hard to overestimate. I hope you also have the holiday's tradition because it leads to the magic moments that bind families and communities together year round.

Traditions are one of the foundations of all families. They are rituals, big or small, that often mark particular times and events throughout the year. Good family traditions give us a sense of belonging and provide ways to express our priorities. They bind us to past generations of family and build a bridge to future ones. Traditions that take place during the winter holiday season are among the most cherished and sacred.

This year you can integrate new ideas for holiday traditions into your life. There are many holiday traditions that you can engage in every year. But, again, it's far less important—especially to kids—what a tradition entails. What's more important is the establishment of holiday rituals, regardless of their form and expectations.

Here are a few ideas for fun and meaningful holiday traditions that you may consider adopting for your own life:

1. Quiet the calendar.

Instead of trying to hit all the parties, all the relatives' houses, all the school functions, and all the city festivities: choose just one per day. Or choose one event per weekend, or one per week, or whatever fits for you and your family best. You aren't missing out because you're creating space for your family to engage with whatever is happening right now fully.

2. Buying a Christmas tree together.

Sure, it's easy to go to the local tree lot and pick up a beautiful artificial tree. But if you make this little event like a family adventure, then the time can be unforgettable.

3. Rethink the gifts.

Winter holidays are a time of celebration and reverence. But what are we celebrating when we spend too much on things we don't need and won't appreciate? What are we giving our energy, time, and money to? And what messages are we sending to the next generations?

There are plenty of alternatives to frenzied holiday shopping:

1) Try to offer just one well-made gift instead of a pile of disposable trinkets.

2) Make handmade gifts, whether that means knitting scarves or redesigning a children's room. You don't have to be an expert in a specific field. Instead, just use the skills you already have to create unique gifts for the people you love.

3) Give real experiences rather than material things. Give your presence to people who have been waiting for it. These are the best

presents for them.

So, instead of exchanging plenty of gifts with loved ones, exchange good deeds.

4. An outdoor adventure.

There is another popular tradition: all gift opening activities on Christmas day must cease by noon. At that point, everyone must wriggle into snow pants, coats, and boots and head outside. People hike, sled, and have snowball fights. They get out in nature and have fun together as a family. (It's amazing how quickly the kids forget about the toys they received while playing and laughing with loved ones in nature.)

5. Try something new.

You really don't have to do things the way you always have. If old tradition has lost its meaning for you, choose something new to try instead. What means the most to you and your family? What will create the memories you want to share? Do that, and let go of the rest.

Try to experience the simple joys of the holidays this year. Too often, the holidays for us look too hectic, full of shopping and social obligations. During the past few years, I've been making a concerted effort to be more mindful, present, and grateful throughout the season while focusing on mosy important things—family, friends, and fun. Once I have read that a big part of mindfulness is maintaining established traditions and creating some new ones. Now I agree with that idea.

Don't get caught up in trying to create perfect, stories-worthy family traditions. Just slow down and let go of expectations. The best traditions are often spontaneous and straightforward. There are no rules when it comes to creating family traditions other than the importance of having them. The real magic of holiday traditions lies in the opportunity to experience unique moments with family that will last for generations to come.

◆ ◆ ◆

CHAPTER 13: WHEN YOUR SPOUSE DON'T FOLLOW SIMPLE LIFE

Sometimes people ask many different questions about the 5 Steps Method and simplicity. But one I find over and over again is, "How can I declutter my life if my husband (or wife) isn't interested?"

I think it's one of the most significant issues people face when they decide to organize their lives. The answers below could apply to a boyfriend or girlfriend or anyone that is an integral part of your life.

If you've had a conversation with your spouse about simplifying your life, and he is not on board, my suggestion is to start with you. Before you start looking at decluttering the kitchen or bedroom, begin in your closet or nightstand.

As you start the process, you will build momentum and be excited to have joy. This is an excellent time to talk to your spouse again.

So, how to talk to your spouse about simplifying:

1. Be a negotiator. Remind your spouse that some decisions are reversible and that if it doesn't work out, you are willing to go back to the way things were. This takes the pressure off some of your simplifying tasks.

2. Focus on the benefits. While cleaning out the bathroom might not sound like a fun way to spend the weekend, when you focus on "why," your husband might come around instead of the how or when. Remind your partner that you can focus more on each other when you don't have to focus on debt and stuff.

3. Daydream together. When you started simplifying your life, you probably thought about how much easier life would be for you and so on. But now it's time to start thinking about how simplifying will help the two of you. How will hoarding less, spending less, working less help you as a couple and as a family? What do you want to do with your time, energy, and lives? What would you differently if you were debt-free? Now is the best chance to dream together.

4. Make your clutter work for your family. If a debt is a part of your relationship, it's time to kick it to the curb. So make your clutter work for you and have a yard sale.

5. Respect the vote. If you want to clean out your closet, go for it right now. But if you want to sell the house, it's time for a vote. Remember: Any big decisions need two and more votes to pass.

6. Hide stuff (start with something very unimportant!). This is not for everyone. But if you think this will work for you, give it a try. Sometimes, decluttering can be a challenge if you share a living space with someone. You own things together, and just because you decide those things don't matter doesn't mean your significant other agrees. So I repeat: Get rid of your own stuff first and often, the other person will join in.

Hiding stuff is a little loophole to leading by example. I am not suggesting that you are sneaky with your spouse or significant other! But there is a way to get rid of your mutual stuff without even having a conversation. Sometimes it's hard to let go of something your partner doesn't really need. Try to hide your partner's stuff (something very unimportant!) and see what she or he thinks after a little time apart.

7. Relationship first of all. Try to notice if your efforts are helping or hurting your relationship. If your actions are causing harm, step back and rethink your approach. Remind your partner that he comes first. If your spouse isn't receptive, focus on your relationship and leave the decluttering for another day.

If these ideas fail at first, do not resort to begging (and definitely no nagging). Instead, simply lead by your example. Continue to declutter your personal possessions and see if there are things you own together, in the bedroom, for example, that your partner would agree to get rid of.

While you might talk to your partner about your decluttering goals and some of the benefits a decluttered life may bring, he or she has to come around. Therefore, it's essential to focus on the benefits and not just the immediate task.

When you married your spouse, in some kind, you married his or her clutter. You married your partner's past and future. But together, it is your responsibility to make your "right now" as good as it can be.

❖ ❖ ❖

CHAPTER 14: HOW TO OFFER 5 STEPS METHOD TO A RELUCTANT SPOUSE OR PARTNER

T hink about it: All of life is offers. Even if we do not offer a product or service, we constantly offer our opinions, worldview, or even what movie we should see on a Friday night. Knowing how to offer an idea to another person is among the most helpful skills anybody can possess.

I think about the reality that much of life is offers—not necessarily offer physical products, but hoping to convince others about our worldview, our political opinion, or even our picture of a perfect weekend with the family.

So, how do we convince a reluctant spouse or partner to adopt a simple lifestyle? Or, better stated, how can we offer the idea of the 5 Steps Method?

1. Put Yourself in Your Counterpart's Shoes.

It's your primary job to figure out your spouse's or partner's motivations. Consider the conversation from their point of view and brainstorm what benefits would draw them to decluttered life. The reason you were drawn to the 5 Steps Method may be different than the reason that would draw them.

They may not feel the weight of cleaning or organizing but may be drawn to the idea of saving money, working less, or having more open space. Find what benefit would move the needle in your family life.

2. Reflect on Your Positive Experiences.

You will not draw a reluctant spouse or partner toward the 5 Steps Method by focusing on the negatives or having the conversation while frustrated.

"You catch more flies with honey than vinegar." —The old proverb.

The old proverbs have stood the test of time because it is true. So, reflect on your own positive experience with simplicity. Don't list the negatives of your partner's current actions. Instead, keep optimism as the foundation for your conversation.

3. Plan, Do and Check.

It is wise to engage in this conversation with your spouse or partner at an appropriate time. Please don't shake your fist in a moment of frustration or rage, and consider that your opportunity to invite him or her into the 5 Steps journey. Too many of our conversations about clutter happen when we are already on edge about our physical possessions.

Think through how you are going to introduce the conversation and practice articulating the benefits that will resonate with your partner. For example, go out for coffee or walking in the park together. Engage in a heartfelt conversation with your spouse about the direction of your lives and what you are hoping to change.

Listen to your partner's intonation as you talk. Try to catch every gesture of him or her. In a word, follow the tone of the conversation. Be wise.

4. Stay Calm in Any Situation.

Humility and selflessness are essential parts of healthy relationships. Therefore, they should be part of this conversation as well.

Be careful not to approach the conversation about the 5 Steps Method with pride and arrogance. Remember, almost certainly, there are a few things your spouse or partner would like to change about you. And I don't think it's unreasonable to assume they may surface during this conversation. So don't get defensive. In fact, your own small weaknesses might be used to your significant advantage if you look for compromise together.

5. Close the Win-Win Deal.

This is important and too often overlooked in offers. End your offer pitch by looking for opportunities to close the deal specifically. Sometimes "closing the win-win deal" means asking your spouse or partner if they are willing to make real change at home. But sometimes, "closing the win-win deal" means something else— especially if they are clearly not ready to jump in with both feet.

"Closing the win-win deal" may be simply asking ourselves, "Is this a conversation you'd be willing to engage in with me in the future?" Or it can be brainstorming ways to work together in the near future or finding an easier first step that he or she is comfortable taking.

6. Think Long-Term Perspective.

It is possible your spouse or partner may not be willing right now to accept simplicity as a lifestyle. Of course, that's too bad, but okay.

Keep leading by your positive example and looking for opportunities in the future to approach the conversation again. Sometimes life change takes much longer than we desire. Show patience. Keep love at the center of your relationship. Think long-term. In the end, the benefits of the 5 Steps Method always win out. Sometimes it just takes a little longer than we hope.

As you may notice from the tips listed above, the key is to be kind, consistent, and purposeful. And then your example will be followed not only by your loved ones but also by all the people around you.

◆ ◆ ◆

CHAPTER 15: HOW TO COMMUNICATE WITH YOUR PARTNER WHEN YOU DISAGREE

You're surfing the blogosphere, and you stumble across several websites on cleaning and simplification. Something in the message resonates deeply in you, and you find yourself prepared to overhaul your home and life. Then the thought hits you: My spouse will never go for it. Now what?

For starters, remember that every relationship has conflicts. And every marriage has conflicts as well, which is why knowing how to communicate with your spouse is so important.

Some problems in marriage are inevitable. The question is—can you remain satisfied in your marriage despite differences? Can your marriage thrive when there are some differences between you?

I believe the answer is "yes." The key is to work it out and grow up continually. Acknowledge the problem and talk about it with your spouse.

In unstable marriages, differences are likely to kill the relationship. And instead of coping, the couple gets gridlocked. People have the same conversation over and over, resolving nothing. And since they're making no progress, they both feel more frustrated, hurt, and rejected.

Problems in marriage will happen anyway. But how you address them is up to you. So here are some ways to communicate better with your partner or spouse when you don't see eye to eye:

1. Be aware of yourself.

To be aware of yourself means you have a deeper awareness and understanding of your beliefs, needs, and desires. And marriage is a great place to clarify these things in your life (mainly because that's the way marriage is designed).

You live with another person who has his or her own view of the way things should be. For example, in your family of origin, tables are great places to eat dinner together, so they need to be free of clutter. But your spouse's family of origin believes tables may serve as great places to store piles of mail, journals, and kid's artwork

Neither way is necessarily "right." Just different. You are allowed to live life the way you choose. But so is your spouse. So be aware of it too.

2. Respect.

One of the main things in couples is a lack of respect. When you reach a point where you no longer like each other, you're in trouble.

> *"Respect is defined as not trying directly or indirectly to change anyone." —Thomas Fogarty*

Sadly, we often treat common strangers with more respect than people in our homes. Yet, respect is one of the key factors to successful and happy relationships—respect for those around you. And most importantly, respect for yourself.

3. Live by what you hold dear.

When you are faced with a situation where you and your partner aren't on the same page, live according to your own integrity and values.

If you want to simplify but your spouse doesn't—simplify only your own life.

You want to eat healthily, but your spouse only wants fast food? Eat healthily and what you want.

Eventually, all you are responsible for is you!

So, when you are faced with something you want to change and have a spouse that isn't on the same page, it's best to initiate a discussion about the change. Share your thoughts and openly listen to theirs. Then, it's very likely that together, you will be able to come up with the best solution.

◆ ◆ ◆

CHAPTER 16: THE BEST TIPS FROM A SIMPLE COUPLES

M oving in together at the start of a happy marriage or as the next step in a committed relationship requires effective communication and compromise. And sharing living space when one is accustomed to managing his or her own space and belongings can be unnerving. Therefore, decisions and plans should be made mutually.

Discussion and acceptance of one another's differences are key. For example, while you may be happy to clear out half of your wardrobe, it is insensitive of you to assume that your partner is willing to do the same or that he will do it as quickly as you would like. Also, one of you may be happy to give everything away, while the other is more enterprising, wanting to try to make a few dollars.

Good planning ahead can help you avoid the chaos and conflict you may have experienced in previous moves. Here are the best tips from simple couples on how the 5 Steps Method can assist with the transition:

1. Declutter as you pack.

When people decide to move in together, they usually have the advantage of time. This allows plenty of time to sort through things and decide what to keep, get rid of, sell and donate.

Even if you are on a tighter schedule with your move, make an effort to eliminate worn-out items and things that you no longer use or need as you are packing. Don't carry the additional physical and emotional weight with you into your new dwelling, thinking you will sort through things once you are settled.

Items bring to mind memories of people and events, some pleasant and some painful, even if you don't recognize them right away. It will be healing to let go of items linked to past relationships in order to start fresh. Not only photos but everyday items can elicit emotional reactions.

Offer your excess, quality items to family and friends. But be careful not to push. Make the offer and if it isn't accepted, donate it. Make the most of the transition time to clear out the old clutter.

2. Be creative.

Walk through the house, room by room, with a list of your furniture in hand to try to determine where things would be placed. Took a careful and deliberate look at each room, what furniture it contained and what pieces you actually liked and needed. Think about using old furniture in different ways or just eliminating the need for some pieces.

3. Remove duplicates.

It's entirely possible that you may both bring the same (or similar items) into your mutual living space. But you may not realize this until you begin to settle into daily life together.

The kitchen and bathroom are locations where a couple will likely have duplicate items. So went through one drawer and one shelf at a time and, when encountering duplicates, decided which one to keep and which one to give away or toss. You will likely repeat this process after more time passes to eliminate items that are not being used.

For example, how many pots and pans do you actually use? How many cups and wine glasses do you really need? You also can box and store extra dishes, glasses, and silverware in the basement for your children.

4. Establish cleaning routines.

The start of a new living arrangement also is a great time to establish new habits. You can agree upon a collection spot in the basement or attic for additional items.

You can also develop your shopping routines. Think about where you will maintain a list: On paper or using an app? How often will you shop and where? With clothing and other belongings, consider a one in, one out approach.

Assign responsibilities and agree on a cleaning schedule. This will help you avoid future misunderstandings.

Soon you will be pleased to report that the 5 Steps approach made what could have been a stressful move into an easy transition for both of you.

All of us face individual challenges, and our opinions vary. But we mutually desire open space, peace, and relaxation time. So why not continue the journey to the perfect home together?

CHAPTER 17: 5 SIMPLE ADVICE FOR NEW FAMILIES

B ecoming a family is an unrivaled experience—and it can be radical. For many people, it has become abundantly clear that time is not forever. Yes, it is also long in some circumstances. But each day that passes is another missed chance to create an extraordinary life. It is too easy to follow the lead of others, becoming distracted by social media, or filling a calendar with too many meetings. As a new family, you have found value in pausing.

Some of the ways I think new families can use this period of intense change are:

1. Find like-minded families.

One of the best ways to cope with a new challenge is to find other families that you can share ideas with and bond with. Of course, it is important to seek out varied opinions, but if it leads to second-guessing yourself, it might pay to find another family to whom you can relate more easily.

Don't break up with your friends, but recognize you need support from family in the way that makes the most sense to you. Having another family with whom you can really be honest is an essential part of staying sane.

2. Let go.

Seeking perfection can be harmful. Always trying to be the perfect family, the perfect spouse, or the perfect employee is a recipe for disaster. A key part of the happiness of a new family is learning to let go of the things that are not important.

There is a difference between what is just urgent and what is most important. Of course, it's up to each family to decide how to prioritize, but many families value good food, rest, exercise, hobbies, time as a family, time as individuals.

3. Just slow down.

By far, one of the most valuable changes you can make is to just slow down. For families, this means saying no to some unimportant events and obligations. It means choosing fewer tasks to complete around the home and being okay with that.

Taking time to find your path through this new stage of life is very important. But, it's equally as important to just enjoy each day and savor the precious moments.

4. Remove distractions.

Social media can be a really powerful tool for connecting people in similar life stages. But it can also take you away from what you already have because it's all too easy to lose several hours scrolling on social media.

No matter your intentions, it happens to all of us. Some of the ways I've found to cope with this are removing the apps from my phone, turning off most notifications, and sometimes leaving them in another room. Sometimes it's not easy. The need to be connected is powerful, and we have become so accustomed to it that it's hard to let it go. But reducing your time on social media will provide a feeling of space and led to less stress.

So pick and choose the times and mediums that work best for you. You can learn more about how to free up your digital space from my previous book:

<u>The 3rd Simple Step to Your Perfect Home: How to Mindfully Clean Your House, Digital, Mind, and Life</u>

5. Embrace the 5 Steps approach.

For some people, having a family does not change their direction. There is no deviation from their set path. But for others, it has completely changed their perspective on life.

Having a new family is a chance to start a new path that will give you more freedom, more energy, and more time. For many people, it is more important than money. As a new family, it can be freeing to embrace the concept of the 5 Steps Method. Get rid of clutter, reduce your consumption, and just live mindfully.

I summarize: Having more time to spend with the ones you love will never be regretted. So, use the 5 Steps Method, free your space, energy, and time and live a happy life!

◆ ◆ ◆

CHAPTER 18: 10 SIMPLE DECLUTTERING SKILLS EVERY PARENT NEEDS

S tuff management is an important life skill—not just for parents, but for kids. Nowadays, parents often stress about how to keep on top of their kids' toys, books, and clothes, neglecting an essential facet of life with kids. But kids can't learn to manage their own stuff if they don't get the practice and support to do so. Children need to learn how to sort through messes and decide themselves what's important to keep and what's not. Then, when kids are grown, we need them to be armed with the skills necessary to manage their possessions, which means we need to help them practice now.

Many parents are overwhelmed trying to manage their own home, let alone the prospect of teaching their children how to declutter and organize their own stuff. But I've found there are only ten simple decluttering skills that parents need to teach their children how to manage their own stuff and set them up for success in the future.

10 Simple Decluttering Skills that Every Parent Need:

1. The willingness to model desired behavior.

Creating a simple lifestyle is not a "do as I say, not as I do" affair. Parents have to be ready and willing to model the lifestyle they want their children to reflect. Kids need to see their parents sorting their own possessions, getting rid of their own clutter, taking responsible care of their own stuff, managing their own tasks and commitments, and prioritizing what's really important—before parents expect to see these traits regularly in their children.

2. A coaching spirit.

Being a "decluttering dictator" isn't going to work well. Demanding that your kids get rid of their stuff isn't going to result in long-term change. Instead, it's just going to generate anger, frustration, and rebellion.

Instead of command, encouragement, thoughtful consideration, and the willingness to coach are keys to teaching kids how to manage their own stuff. We need to instill good habits that can last a lifetime, not just temporary "my house, my rules" behavior.

3. The willingness to provide needed resources (including books and supplies).

Sometimes things are needed to help the decluttering process along, whether it's boxes and trash bags or an excellent how-to book (I hope a book like this).

Maybe it's access to a blog with decluttering encouragement. Perhaps it's a few minutes on the phone with a trusted mentor. It might even be a few new supplies to organize that beloved collection your child wants to keep tidy.

Keeping an open mind to what your child is asking for to help them get the job done helps build trust that you're a partner in the decluttering process.

4. The ability to distinguish between a "want" and a "need."

A crucial part of decluttering and simplifying is the ability to determine what actually constitutes a "need" versus what items fall under the category of "wants." Sometimes it can be challenging to tell them apart sometimes, particularly for children and teens. The basic idea of shelter, food, and clothing as needs is not as black and white as it may seem.

Yes, clothing is necessary, but are designer jeans really need? What about a fashionable jacket? And new shoes? A cell phone may be a need for teens with lots of extracurricular activities in some families, but is a smartphone a need or a want for your kid?

Without a doubt, it depends on the individual lifestyle and preferences of the family. Needs versus wants will be different for each family, and it's up to parents to decide what falls into each category (not just for kid's stuff but for their stuff as well).

5. The desire to ask the right questions.

Decluttering and organizing isn't about just tossing everything that isn't needed. Instead, it's about looking at items with the intention of keeping what is useful and fulfilling.

The questions must don't stop at "do you use or wear this right now?" That's too simplistic, especially for kids who still place emotional value on material objects.

Decluttering has to be tailored to suit the kid's personality and headspace. And you need to be willing to go beyond the straightforward "are you still using this" question. Other questions to consider include:

1) Do you use this regularly?

2) Does it help you feel comfortable?

3) What feelings do you have when you hold this item?

4) Does this item make you happy?

5) How would you feel if this item was gone?

6. The willingness sometimes to stay hands-off and leave your children to decide themselves.

As difficult as it can be, kids need to be in the driver's seat when it comes to managing their own stuff, particularly as they get older. Obviously, tiny tots and preschoolers need lots of help. But older kids and teens need the respect and responsibility of deciding for themselves how to manage their possessions.

So if you're modeling the behavior you wish to instill and helping your kids ask the right questions when it comes to making choices about what to keep and what to let go of, you have to trust that your kids can make the best decisions for themselves.

7. The ability to listen.

Sometimes kids don't know what to do with their things. Particularly if they have a lot of stuff and have never really processed what it feels like to let go of things voluntarily. As a result, they may be overwhelmed, sad, and feel anxious.

All those feelings are totally fine and expected, and kids need to know that it's OK to feel whatever they feel as they learn to manage their own possessions.

As a parent, it's crucial to sit with them and just listen to your kids without judging what they're feeling or saying. They need that safe space with you to learn to process their feelings. In addition, material possessions are often tied to memories, so kids are often anxious about losing a memory if they let go of an item associated with it. And your presence can help them cope with this.

8. The ability to explain.

It's more easy to let things go when you have some choices on how to get rid of them. Part of decluttering process is learning how to discard responsibly. Showing kids that they have options for how to let go of things can help them feel good with the decision of letting their stuff go.

Things that still have use left may be given to relatives or friends. Maybe there's a charity in town or homeless shelter that can use your child's discards. Maybe a church or hospital can use some toys for their nurseries. Maybe your child would like to try to sell a few things on a local buy/sell group or a yard sale to earn some extra spending money. Maybe your children's books can go to the city library or a school or preschool library.

Things that may no longer be useful sometimes may be able to be recycled instead of trashed bound for a landfill. Giving your child options for how to get rid of their stuff may make things a little more complicated at first. But in the long term, it can make them feel good about their choice to simplify and to feel fulfilled knowing their discards can go to helping others feel cared for. And to become a good example, donate some of your things to charities. Children love to imitate their parents.

9. Except when hand-on assistance is really needed.

There is a time for parents to back off and a time to get involved. And when help is really needed, parents need to be willing to step in and offer the assist.

The chances are good that your child will want your help with their stuff at some point. The critical skill is the ability to help without feeling the need to jump in and take over. Sometimes kids need guidance and mentoring, but they don't need us to jump in and do it for them.

So, if you see your child struggling with managing his stuff, you can offer to help. Not say, "I'll just do it for you," but ask if he would like a helping hand, either with decisions, the manual work of cleaning, or both.

It's tough to even for adults to declutter their stuff, so kids can't be expected to do everything independently. So let them take the lead and be willing to help them navigate the complex feelings that come with simplifying their possessions.

10. The patience.

There's no doubt about it—decluttering and learning to live an organized lifestyle requires patience. Rooms don't become cluttered overnight, so it's unrealistic to expect everything to be clean and clutter-free in just a few hours.

Being patient with your child as he or she learns this new skill. With time encouraging a kid to keep working at it will help both of you feel good about the progress both of you are making.

If you can develop all skills mentioned above, your kids will be way ahead of most. So this is not only your child's work—it is your joint practice of living a clutter-free life.

◆ ◆ ◆

CHAPTER 19: THE 5 STEPS METHOD FOR MOMS

For moms, the 5 Steps Method originally seems an unobtainable goal. They thought the 5 Steps approach either traveled the globe with a single backpack of belongings or had a home with a futon and a single vase on a table (if they even had a table). But, of course, that kind of simplicity works for some people, and I think that's cool. That kind of freedom must be really impressive. But this is not necessary at all!

Can the 5 Steps approach really be applied to a family with kids? Not only can but also will be very useful. But sometimes, we jump to conclusions that talk us out of starting. So let's start with what organized mommy doesn't need to look like.

Organized Mommy is Not:

Getting rid of all the toys in the house.

Throwing out all the family photos.

Owning just one pair of shoes.

Selling television, car, and couch.

When I dove deeper into the 5 Steps Method and saw the many different ways people were applying simplicity to their lives, I was greatly encouraged. I began actually to believe that the 5 Steps approach could work for everyone. As I started on my own journey towards organized life, my enthusiasm grew, and everywhere I looked, I saw where it was desperately needed.

Soon I began to see the many areas of excess where the 5 Steps method could make a real difference:

Kitchens were full of useless gadgets and extra items that never get touched.

Toys were spilling out of bedrooms and taking over living rooms.

Drawers of kid clothes so packed that nothing else would fit.

Families that never seem to have any time spent together because they are all busy doing their own thing.

Many of these I saw in my own life and home. There is just so much excess everywhere—excess words, excess possessions, and excess scheduling. It's time for decluttering! The 5 Steps approach doesn't have to mean getting rid of everything. It is simply a tangible way of organizing the things that are important and getting rid of the rest.

If you are wishing things could be different, then just ask yourself, "What can I do today to get to where I want to be?" Of course, you can't do everything by yourself, but there is actually a lot that we can control and bring back some balance to the family.

So, what can you do just today?

If you want a more cleaned-out closet, get rid of the clothes you haven't worn.

If you want a cleaner, more organized kitchen, go throw away a few of the gadgets you haven't touched in months.

If you want fewer toys to pick up, walk over to the toy box and start going through those toys.

If you want to make some family memories, cancel the plans for this weekend and spend it together as a family.

Each family is different, and every journey is unique. So tap into your power as a mom and accomplish something significant for your family today. And start right now.

◆ ◆ ◆

CHAPTER 20: HOW TO GET CLUTTERFREE WITH KIDS

The clutterfree life holds benefits for all. But, unfortunately, numbers of parents think a clutterfree lifestyle is simply out of reach because they have children—as if the two are somehow incompatible. But that is really not the case. As I explain in the previous chapters of this book, the principles of clutterfree are completely within reach no matter how many children you have or where you live.

And not only is simplicity completely possible with children, but it is also a lifestyle filled with benefits for them! Since becoming clutterfree, I have been continually amazed at some of the lessons I have learned from simple families.

Over the past years, I have learned from simple families:

* That we really don't need to live life like everyone else. Even though sometimes we are not quite old enough to understand all of the intricacies of our clutterfree life, we can completely understand that we have made a decision to live differently than most people.

* That we can live within our means. Although children are not balancing our checkbooks, they can hear their parents often speak about debt, the joy of not being in it, and their desire to stay out of it.

* That we don't really need to buy things to be happy. We can own far fewer things than we did years ago. We can purchase far fewer

things than we did years ago. Yet, we can be far happier than we were years ago. Go figure.

* That we think carefully about new purchases. We need to buy things like toys, school supplies, art supplies, and sporting goods. But we can think through our buying decisions more carefully. We can no longer buy something just because we have the money. We can buy things because we truly need them. This is an invaluable lesson for kids to learn as they get older.

* That we can gladly share with others. Since we can become clutterfree when kids are young, they have grown up watching us donate many of our belongings to others. So they have seen generosity in action.

* That clutter is a distraction. Kids can see how clutter distracts parents from what really matters. And when it does show up, it can be quickly remedied with the help of a clutterfree lifestyle.

* That we can have more free time. Clutterfree homes allow us the opportunity to spend less time purchasing, cleaning, organizing, and sorting things. So we can replace that time managing stuff with spending time with kids.

To get clutterfree with kids is entirely possible. However, it does require a little more motivation, a little more thoughtfulness, and a little more patience. **So, as you embark or continue on the clutterfree journey with your kids, here are some practical steps to consider:**

1. Clearly explain your decision.

Your kids are thinking human beings. Therefore, no matter their age, sit down and explain your decision to them—include the reasons you are choosing to become clutterfree and the benefits your family is hoping to receive from it. And because teenagers typically jump to far-reaching conclusions, assure them that your decision does not mean you will no longer buy anything. Instead, it just means you are going to think through your purchases in the future more intentionally.

2. Begin sorting your possessions first.

Start sorting your personal belongings first and your shared family belongings second. It would be unfair to ask your child/teenager to adopt the clutterfree lifestyle until you have done it personally thoroughly. Also, remember, you will learn valuable lessons when you remove your personal clutter—valuable lessons that will put you in a better place to help your son or daughter navigate their own journey.

* I recommend you do everything step-by-step and follow the instructions in the first book in the 5 Step series:

The 1st Simple Step to Your Perfect Home: How to Methodologically Sort Through All Items, Keep Important, and Get Rid of Unnecessary

3. Remove the items your kids do not use.

Clutterfree process is about paring down to only the essentials. It is about removing the things in our life we don't need more so we can focus on the things that we do. And while most homes are filled with old things that are not needed, they are also filled with things that are not even used. So you can begin by removing the clothes your kids no longer wear, the toys they no longer play with, and the other things they no longer use. That's a fundamental step. As you begin there and talk them through the process, kids may begin to naturally start asking themselves the question, "How much of this other stuff do I really need anyway?"

4. Focus on the positives.

As you begin to see the benefits of clutterfree life for your children, point them out and focus on them. Just because you are observant enough to notice them doesn't mean they see it quite as readily as you.

Do they spend less time tidying?

Does their room appear cleaner?

Is it easier to find things?

Can you notice less stress and fewer distractions?

Are you more relaxed?

Encourage each other with the positive benefits that you notice in lives.

5. Treat them to fun experiences.

One benefit of a clutterfree lifestyle is that you spend less and have more time on your hands. So you should have some extra disposable income and the time to do something with it. Now you can use it to create fun, family experiences. Do something new that everyone in your family will enjoy. You don't need to spend all of your newfound savings on this event (especially if you are trying to get out of debt in the process). But a practical, fun experience that highlights the benefits of your decision can go a long way in helping your children understand your clutterfree decision.

6. Choose your purchases carefully.

You will still need to buy things. Kids will outgrow their toys, their clothes, their school supplies, and their sporting goods. They are not going to stop developing. You are absolutely still going to buy things going forward. You are just going to put more thought into your purchases than you did in the past. Replace "Do we want this?" with "Do we need this?" And help your son or daughter ask the same question regularly. It's one of the most important lessons they will ever learn in life.

7. Buy gifts wisely.

Parents desire to show their love by giving gifts, and their children feel loved when they receive them. Parents don't want to take that this tradition away from their families. However, we have to do what we can to communicate with our families ahead of time and ask them about things they need prior to birthdays and holidays.

8. Be patient.

Be patient with your family as much as possible. Offer them plenty of time to adjust to a clutterfree lifestyle rather than being pushed into it. Clutterfree is a lifestyle that needs to be believed in and adopted. Show your kids plenty of patience. And after all, if it took you 35 years to discover and adopt this lifestyle, it would be foolish to assume they will fully adopt it in 35 minutes (or even 35 days).

Let me assure you: Clutterfree approach is completely achievable and beneficial for you and your family. You just need to start.

◆ ◆ ◆

CHAPTER 21: WHY FEWER TOYS WILL BENEFIT YOUR CHILDREN

Kid's toys are not merely playthings. Instead, toys form the building blocks for our child's future life. They teach children about themselves and the world around them. And thus, wise parents think about what foundation is being laid by the toys that are given to their children.

Wise parents also think about the number of toys that kids are given. While most toy rooms and bedrooms today are filled to the ceiling with toys, intentional parents learn to limit the number of toys that their children have to play with.

They understand that fewer toys and practicing simple life will actually benefit their children in the long term:

1. Children live in a tidier home.

If you have kids, you know that toy clutter can quickly take over an entire home. But fewer toys result in a less-cluttered, cleaner, tidier home.

2. Children develop longer attention spans.

When too many toys are introduced into a kid's life, their attention span will begin to suffer. In addition, kids will rarely learn to fully appreciate the toy in front of them when there are countless options still remaining on the shelf behind them.

3. Children learn to find satisfaction outside of the toy store.

True joy, contentment, and happiness will never be found in the aisles of a toy store. Unfortunately, children who have been raised to think the answer to their desires can be bought with money have believed the same lie as their parents. Instead, children need encouragement to live simple lives finding joy in things that truly last.

4. Children experience more of nature.

Kids who do not have a basement full of toys are more apt to play outside and develop a deep appreciation for nature. They are also more likely to be involved in physical exercise, which results in healthier and happier bodies.

5. Children develop a greater love for reading, writing, and art.

Fewer toys allow your kids to love books, music, and painting. In turn, a love for art will help them better appreciate beauty, emotion, and communication in their world. It'll also keep them away from getting used to an unhealthy amount of screen time and develop creativity.

6. Children learn to be more creative.

Too many toys prevent kids from fully developing their inner gift of imagination. Two German public health workers (Strick and Schubert) conducted an important experiment. They convinced a kindergarten classroom to remove all of their toys for three months. Although boredom set in during the initial stages of the investigation, the children soon began to use their basic surroundings to invent games and use imagination in their playing.

7. Children become more resourceful.

In education, students aren't just given the answer to a problem. They are given the tools to find the proper answer. In everyday life and work, the same principle can be applied. Fewer toys cause children to become resourceful by solving problems with only the materials at hand. In turn, resourcefulness is a gift with unlimited potential.

8. Children learn to take greater care of things.

When children have too many toys, they will naturally take less care of them. They will not learn to value their toys if there is always a replacement ready at hand. So if you have a child who is constantly damaging their toys—just take a bunch away. Your kid will quickly learn.

9. Children learn determination and patience.

Kids who have too many toys give up too quickly. If they have a toy that they can't figure out, it will soon be discarded for the sake of a different, easier one. But children with fewer toys learn determination, perseverance, and patience.

10. Children become less selfish.

Children who get everything they want believe they can have everything they want. Unfortunately, this attitude will quickly lead to an unhealthy lifestyle and relationships.

11. Children argue with each other less.

Many parents believe that more toys will result in less fighting because there are more options available for kids. However, the opposite is true far too often! Siblings and best friends sometimes argue about toys. And every time we introduce a new toy into the relationship between kids, we give them another reason to establish their "territory" among the others. On the other hand, siblings with fewer toys are forced to share, collaborate, and play together.

12. Children establish better communication skills.

Kids with fewer toys learn how to develop interpersonal relationships with other kids and adults. They begin to learn the give and take of a good conversation. Studies have attributed childhood friendships to a greater chance of success academically and in social situations during adulthood. And better relationships as a child also tend to lead happier lives in adulthood.

I'm not anti-toy (I had enough toys in my childhood). But I'm just pro-balance. So do your kids a favor today and limit their number of toys.

P. S. Just don't tell them you got the idea from me ;)

◆ ◆ ◆

CHAPTER 22: A STEP-BY-STEP GUIDE FOR DECLUTTERING TOYS WITH YOUR CHILDREN

K id's toys. Sometimes, they feel like they are everywhere. But to be fair, the exact "ideal number" of toys will vary from family to family. Hopefully, each of the following tips will be helpful to those of you who know the ideal number is certainly less than you have today.

1. Be convinced that less is better.

As with any simplifying project, it always begins with a heartfelt belief that less is better and desirable. I'm assuming if you have read past the chapters of this book, you already believe this to be true when it comes to toys.

2. Fewer toys are different than no toys.

Toys can be educational and play an essential role in a child's development. Just to be clear, I'm not advocating any toys. I'm arguing for balance.

3. Prepare your children to make conscious choices.

Involve your kids in the toy purging process. Help them make conscious decisions about which toys should stay and which should go. This also will serve them well into adulthood.

4. Clean and organize toys with your kids.

Most likely, you need to make a clean sweep of your childrens' toys right now. Removing the toys that are no longer used is a great place to start and shouldn't take too long. First, put the clean, unused toys in boxes and store them in the attic or basement. (If your children do not need toys for a long time, you can donate them to a homeless shelter, medical center, nonprofit organization, local church, or orphanage.) Then simply discard the broken ones. And stay on top of the clutter by cleaning and organizing on a regular basis with your kids.

5. Set a physical space for children's toys.

Whether it is a container, a shelving unit, or a closet—set a confined physical space for your children's toys. And once the space is full, there is no room to add more toys. Help your kids understand that principle by clearly marking the boundaries. If they want to add new toys (think after birthdays or holidays), they'll need to remove old ones first.

6. Realize your own motivation for purchasing toys.

Most kids don't buy toys for themselves—somebody else does. So if there are too many toys in your home, start with yourself. Ask yourself: Why are there so many toys in my home? A healthy look at your own motivations may go a long way in solving this issue.

7. Limit your purchasing with a budget.

If your budget for other categories in your life (groceries, clothing, entertainment), you already understand how this principle can help keep your spending and consumption in check. If you don't, start today by setting a weekly/monthly/yearly budget for toys. Enforcing a predetermined budget amount will help in limiting kid's toy purchases.

8. Limit the screen time for your kids.

Consider the fact that marketers are brilliant at shaping the desires of men and women (young and old). Now, imagine giving them hours each day to shape your children's minds too. Soon you'll quickly realize that you don't stand a chance. So make sure to limit the screen time for your kids. (A whole chapter of this book will be devoted to this topic.)

9. Keep a realistic attitude toward toy companies and toy stores.

They may tell you that their main goal is to help or educate your child. But often times, they are driven mostly by their bottom line.

10. Don't give in to your kid's temper tantrums at the store.

Every time you give in to a temper tantrum at the store just to avoid a scene, you encourage your child to do it again. As a result, they quickly learn how to manipulate you. So don't worry about the scene that is taking place in public. Wise parents in the store will respect you for not giving in (and not-so-wise parents will learn a valuable lesson).

11. Don't give into fads.

Toy companies will generate a new "toy-fad" every few months by artificially generating a cultural buzz. And if done well, this artificial buzz will become mainstream in the culture and no longer feel artificial. But it will always pass. So you don't need to give into cultural buzz just because every other parent is.

12. Avoid duplicate toys.

Encourage your children to explore all the toys they have (sometimes kids do not remember which toys they already have). Instead of buying duplicates, require your kids to learn the invaluable life lessons of generosity, sharing, cooperation, and compromise.

13. Choose quality over quantity.

You and your kids will benefit more from toys that are chosen for their quality (in workmanship) and purpose (playability) than for their sheer quantity. And just like everything else in life, too many toys will always distract from the significant ones.

14. Teach kids to value other activities.

Although all kids have natural tendencies towards specific endeavors, expand their minds by regularly introducing them to new activities that don't revolve around toys.

15. Be an example and limit your toys too.

Children will always learn more from example than words. So if your life is caught up in always needing to own the latest technology, fashion, or product on the market, theirs will be too. And it would be unreasonable to expect anything else.

Keeping fewer toys always requires thought and intentionality. But it also will always result in your children learning to value who they are more than what they have. So that always makes it worth the effort.

◆ ◆ ◆

CHAPTER 23: CREATING A SIMPLE WARDROBE FOR KIDS

I think every parent knows there are mountains of laundry involved with kids. The secret to getting through this is creating a simple wardrobe inspired by the 5 Steps Method. The goal is to optimize kid's clothing in your house in order to make laundry day and getting dressed much more simple.

Why have a simple wardrobe? In a simple wardrobe, each piece is carefully and intentionally chosen. Ideally, your entire wardrobe would consist of articles of clothing that are comfortable, fit well, and can be mixed.

This takes the stress out of dressing in the morning and ensures you're never standing in a crowded closet feeling like there is "nothing to wear." Sounds great, doesn't it?

I talked in more detail about how to organize the simple wardrobe in one of my previous books:

The 2nd Simple Step to Your Perfect Home: How to Methodically Put All Necessary Items in the Optimal Places and Organize Everyday Life

But does a simple wardrobe really work for kids? Yes, even considering that it can be difficult trying to stay on top of both the daily outfit changes and constantly changing sizes as kids grow.

Therefore the criteria for kid's simple wardrobes might look different than it does for adults.

For example, you might be less worried about style and investment pieces and more about what fits them and can be cleaned very easily. Here are some criteria for choosing which pieces to use for your child's simple wardrobe project.

1. Make a laundry schedule.

If you're worried that after decluttering items won't be enough, make a laundry schedule. This might seem like an odd step, to begin with. But think about how often you do laundry and then work around this. For example, if you do laundry once a week, then you'll obviously need at least a week's worth of clothing. Your kid's items have to cover that schedule (even with extra outfit changes during the day).

If you find yourself doing laundry twice a week, you might get away with having less (or you'll have even more options). But, even if you don't have set times to do laundry, think about implementing a schedule to become more organized. You'll discover that the 5 Steps Method can fit a lifestyle with children.

2. Separate off-season items.

Eliminate the chaos of having everything in the closet at once. Only keep the items for this season, and then separate and store any off-season clothes. You can use a big bin which will sit on the top shelf in the closet. This also applies to any clothes that they will grow into soon.

However, don't get carried away with storing for seasons; otherwise, this will become another source of the extra clutter. Depending on the climate you live in, perhaps organizing twice per year could be enough: a Fall/Winter season and Spring/Summer season.

3. Keep tops and bottoms that mix.

If you have too much and are trying to pare down, I suggest you keep items that easily mix and match with each other. You can do this by choosing pants that go with most of the tops: khakis, jeans, or colors that match a lot of existing items.

When everything goes together, it makes it simple to grab a top and a bottom. And if you have kids who insist on dressing themselves, then you have the added bonus: they'll actually pick things that match.

4. Pass on extra clothing.

Every person might approach this differently, but I recommend giving away clothes as soon as your children grow out of them. One way that clutter accumulates quickly in homes is when we keep items "just in case."

You are lucky enough if you have a lot of people give you second-hand clothes for your kids. In this case, you can buy clothes only when there's a gap in their wardrobe, and a specific item is needed. If you are given so much, you probably like to pass on things to other people too.

I think it is better to give items to someone who definitely needs them now than keep things for my own "someday, maybe."

5. Keep kid's closets simple.

I recommend keeping the kids' clothing in bins instead of a dresser. For example, each child could have:

1) One box for underwear (including bathing suit and socks);

2) One box for tops (cardigans, sweaters, and T-shirts);

3) One box for bottoms (dresses, pants, and shorts);

4) And one box for pajamas.

So, instead of hanging or folding kid's clothes, you could simply sort the clean clothes into the correct box. This makes it easy to put clean clothes away and easy to find things early in the morning (especially when you harry). And when you move the boxes onto the floor, the kids can sort their own clean laundry.

Make some free space in your closets, house, and family life. Apply the 5 Steps Method to your child's clothing and see how simplicity can make your family's life organized and calmer.

◆ ◆ ◆

CHAPTER 24: 10 IMPORTANT STRATEGIES FOR RAISING CHILDREN FREE FROM TECHNOLOGY CLUTTER

M y generation, it seems, had the last of the truly low-tech childhoods. And now we are among the first of the truly high-tech people.

But when it comes to parenting, I think this statement extremely uncomfortable because I know what childhood and adolescence were like before the Internet. But our next generation will not know it.

Parents today know the decisions they make for their kids concerning technology are important—but entirely without context. But a conversation about nowadays technology addiction is one we should be having. Too much technology in our lives can easily transform into high-tech clutter.

So here are 10 important strategies we can implement raising children in an age of technology:

1. Technology is not primary in our homes.

Technology, it appears, is going to be around for quite a while. Our next generations will need the high-tech skills in the future—they already do in the present. Parenting is not about shielding children from the tools of the world but equipping them to use those tools wisely.

We should be active and intentional in teaching them how to use technology properly and to its fullest potential. In practical terms, this means conduct conversations with children about the importance of technology in our lives and tell them how to find the right balance between virtual and real life.

2. Technology increases the opportunity for distractions.

From leaving hard conversations, procrastinating important work, or losing the ability to self-reflect, technology represents an ever-present temptation to leave difficult places. Those who will succeed in the future will be the ones who learn to overcome this temptation successfully.

3. Moderation is encouraged.

While we know very little about the future of technology and how it might look, we do have ample study on the effects of screen time on kids. For example, studies have shown that excessive media use can lead to attention problems, sleep and eating disorders, and school difficulties.

Most recently, The American Academy of Pediatrics recommends television and other entertainment media should be avoided entirely for children under age 2. Also, to help kids make wise media choices, parents should monitor their media diet for both content and duration.

4. Age restrictions on technology.

The minimum age for most social networks is 13 years old. Therefore, parents should not allow their kids to have accounts on those networks before the minimum age limit is reached.

While some kids under the age of 13 may be mature enough to use the networks wisely, there is a more significant issue at play—honesty. When parents allow their children to misrepresent their age/identity solely for the purpose of gaining access, they set a dangerous precedent for the future.

5. We shouldn't believe everything we see on the Internet.

The Internet could use more fact-checkers—though we are not overly concerned about this. Far more damaging are the profiles we create representing ourselves online. We post our most glorious moments online but hide the most painful. We deliberately build a facade of happiness, success, and an image of having it all together. But inside, sometimes, we are as lost and broken.

Our online selves need more authenticity and truth. And children need to know the danger of comparing themselves to the rose-colored profiles created on social media.

6. Self-worth can not be calculated by likes, shares, and retweets.

The praise of other people is a fickle thing upon which to measure our worth. It is an ever-changing target. It often negatively impacts our decisions and the life we choose to live, but it never fully satisfies our hearts. So it is vital for kids to understand their self-worth must be found elsewhere. And it is equally vital for us as adults to learn the same.

7. A face-to-face conversation is still important in the present (and will likely be important in the future).

Technology is changing the way we relate to one another. Nowadays, technology is permanently changing the way we communicate—whether it is for the better or not remains to be seen. Older generations will argue technology is destroying conversation.

Younger generations will argue technology is enhancing it. But only time will tell.

Either way, the next generations will forever live in a world where their immediate elders respect and expect verbal conversation. Our future generations may value it less. But in the meantime, for children to be successful in communicating with older generations, they must be able to communicate both online and in person. So we should create safe opportunities where they can learn.

8. Technology is fickle.

Excites things will turn out to be an unnecessary trinket tomorrow. So in our time, it is very important to learn to resist the majority of false advertising campaigns, the purpose of which is to sell you a new product.

It is crucial to teach children to understand the difference between advertising for technologies that are changing the world and intrusive advertising that seeks to impose their opinions on us.

9. Technology must serve a purpose.

Technology should solve problems. Purchasing technology purely for the sake of owning technology is a fool's gold and has run countless others into great debt. When it comes to buying technology, we need routinely ask ourselves, "What problem does it solve?"

Technology should make our lives easier and more efficient. So if a new technology is not solving an existing problem, it is only adding to them.

10. Technology can be used for consumption or creation.

We should choose creation whenever possible. This is, perhaps, one of the most important distinctions concerning technology that we can teach our next generations. We can browse social networks, or we can create places and communities that serve a purpose. We can play video games, or we can create them. There is a place in our world for technological consumption, but creation trumps consumption every day as an approach to life. Help your children understand the difference.

Like any area of life, parenting requires a healthy balance of humility and fierce resolve. Are there any essential strategies you have implemented with your kids that you think are important to add?

◆ ◆ ◆

CHAPTER 25: HOW WISELY TO REDUCE YOUR CHILD'S SCREEN TIME

The next stats illustrate a frightening trend when it comes to screen time for kids:
* Kids under age 6 watch an average of about 2 hours of screen media a day (primarily TV and videos or DVDs).

* Counting all media outlets, 8 to 18 year-olds devote an average of 7 hours and 38 minutes to using entertainment media across a typical day.

* Kids and teens 8 to 18 years spend nearly 4 hours a day in front of a TV screen and almost 2 additional hours on the computer (outside of schoolwork) and playing video games.

And often, the effects of television, or any technology addiction, on children are not good. Children who watch too much television:

* Are more likely to display aggressive behavior because children naturally copy what they see (and as you know, basically all programs are related to violence on TV).

* Are more exposed to advertisements, propaganda, and commercials.

* Are more likely to engage in "risky behaviors" when they get older.

Most people would agree with research that our culture watches too much. Yet, only a few people are able to curb their habit and reclaim their life. And even fewer know how to wisely help their children navigate the media-drenched world we live in.

Here are 10 tips to help limit screen time for your kids:

1. Observe Your Child's Behavioral Changes. Without a doubt, television has an immediate impact on your child's behavior. After too much television or video games, children get irritable, aggressive, impatient, and selfish. Be on the lookout for these behavioral changes. When you start to notice them yourself, you'll probably be less inclined to put your kids in front of the screen.

2. Just Be the Parent. It is your job to encourage healthy behaviors and limit unhealthy ones. And sometimes, this means making unpopular decisions like limiting your children's screen time. But make these tough decisions for your children. And always go to the next step of explaining why you have made the decision. This will help them follow through and someday choose it for themselves.

3. Set Limited Viewing Times. Instead of a turn off the television completely, choose the appropriate television viewing windows for your kids. It is much easier to limit their viewing habit if they understand that they can only watch one show in the morning and one show in the evening (as just an example).

4. Cut your Cable or Remove Your Television Completely (but first consult with your spouse). If you really want a sure-fire way to limit your child's television viewing habits, cut your cable/satellite television feed (or just remove your television completely). This step will change your family's life overnight. By the way, it will positively impact your checkbook too.

5. Don't Worry if Your Kid Miss Out on Parts of the Conversations with Friends. Your child's friend will often talk about television. They will compare notes about cartoons or prime-time programming. Maybe you will think that you are depriving your child of friendships because they can not join in on those parts of the conversation. But don't worry! You will have successfully prepared your child to enter into far more profound, richer conversations than the most recent episode of the morning show.

6. Be Involved in Your Kid's Lives. For many parents, it is just easier to turn on the television than to actually be involved in the lives of their children. But those intimate life details are so required for successful parenting. So observe, ask, and listen.

7. Value Family Meals. About two-thirds of young people say the TV is usually on during meals. That's too bad because your family's richest conversations will always take place during meals. So value those times with your kids and don't let the TV steal them from you. Be present with your family.

8. Play with Your Kids. Get down on the floor with your kids and pick up a doll, ball, or truck. It takes intentionality and selfless love when they are 4. But when they turn 14, you'll be glad you did.

9. Encourage Other Hobbies. Provide the necessary resources for your kids: books to read, board games, art supplies, and sporting equipment. Ask your child what activities he or she would like to do at the moment.

10. Set the Right Example. Start with the toughest one because children will always gravitate toward the modeled behaviors of their parents. For example, if they see you reading a book, they are more likely to read too. And if they see you watching television, so will they follow your example.

Limiting your child's screen time may seem like an impossible chore. Also, it may seem like a battle that is too difficult to fight. But this is not a battle—this is a compromise.

Implementing just a few steps right away will help you implement the others. And the more you turn your TV off, the easier it becomes to keep it off and limit the screen time for kids. You've just got to start someday.

◆ ◆ ◆

CHAPTER 26: 7 SIMPLE LESSONS WE CAN LEARN FROM KIDS

K ids add joy, purpose, and fulfillment to our lives. They also bring us smiles, optimism, and cheerful attitudes. And given a chance, they will teach us valuable life lessons.

"While we try to teach our children all about life, our children teach us what life is all about." —Angela Schwindt

Certainly, growing children (physically, socially, intellectually, and emotionally) have added a new dimension to our life journey, but we wouldn't want it any other way. In fact, some of the most important lessons about life and simplicity have been learned by watching children.

Consider these 7 Simple Lessons We Can Learn From Kids:

1. Life's pains are healed best by a hug and a kiss.

Kids fall down very often. And when they fall, they only want one thing—their mommy to pick them up, give a kiss, and tell them that everything is going to be okay. They don't ask for a new toy or videogame. They only desire love and security. They have found the universal antidote to pain and wouldn't trade it for anything else.

Life lesson: Don't look towards material things to soothe the pain we encounter in life. Instead, seek acceptance, love, and security.

2. Fancy possessions and character are entirely unrelated.

Kindergarten and First Grade may be the only places left on earth where labels don't exist. At age 7, everyone is accepted, and everyone plays with everyone else. Each child starts the day on equal footing. And nobody is pre-judged by the house that they live in or the clothes that they wear.

Life lesson: Respect people by their hearts and character, not by the meaningless externals of life.

3. Clothes are not worn to impress others.

Little kids don't wear clothes to impress other people. I don't think the idea of trying to impress others by wearing the latest fashions has ever crossed their minds. They feel no pressure to conform or impress.

Simple lesson: Wear clothing for its usefulness rather than as an attempt to impress others.

4. Too many new toys in a box only get in the way of the good ones.

A funny thing happens after the holiday—a mountain of new toys enters childrens' lives. The joy of new toys reigns at homes. However, after two or three days, they are pushed to the side as kids return to the tried-and-true toys they had been playing with long before the holiday ever occurred. The new toys we thought would make them happier don't. Opposite, they just start to get in the way.

Life lesson: We often think that material possessions will bring lasting excitement into our lives. But most of the time, they just end up getting in the way.

5. The more toys you play with, the more time you spend cleaning them up.

When kids clean up toys every night before bed, they understand this pretty simple equation. The more toys they pull out of the closet, the more time they spend cleaning them up. And conversely, the less time they spend actually enjoying them.

Life lesson: The more possessions we own, the more of our time is required to care for them, clean them, sort and organize them.

6. One neighborhood friend is worth more than a basement full of new toys.

Kids can spend countless hours with their neighborhood friends running from yard to yard, catching bugs, or swinging on swings. They can easily spend every afternoon and evening together without being bored. But take them away from their friends for one Saturday at home with their toys, and boredom almost immediately sets in. Yes, the joy of playing alone in a roomful of toys quickly fades.

Simple lesson: Relationships with others are always more exciting and fulfilling than possessions.

7. A hike in the park beats a new video game any day.

Video games simply can not compete with the graphics, the full-sensory experience, or the relationship of a family walk through the park. Also, for that matter, nothing else produced on television can compete either. Never have, and never will.

Life lesson: Turn off the TV. Take a walk. Live life, don't just watch it.

Perhaps kids are in this world because we as grown-ups have so much left to relearn. And they can teach us how to live fully.

◆ ◆ ◆

CHAPTER 27: 15 GENERAL CLUTTER-BUSTING ROUTINES FOR ANY FAMILY

A s I mentioned in previous chapters, several years ago, I decided to pursue simple, clutter-free life. At my first step, I have tried to remove all of the possessions from my home that are not essential. In doing so, I have found new opportunities to spend my time, energy, and finances on the most important things to me.

Also, I became far more observant about how my family's items rob us of our precious freedom. We have learned that just like most families, no matter how hard we try to stop it, stuff inevitably continues to enter our homes.

So we work hard to remove any clutter that begins to accumulate in our homes and lives. Along the way, we have picked up some general clutter-busting routines to help those who are just getting started with clutter-free living.

Here are 15 clutter-busting routines we have found helpful in our homes:

1. Spend a little time (5-10 minutes) daily keeping order in your home.

Keep your home tidy every day. Bedroom dressers, tabletops, kitchen counters, bathroom counters—after you clear them the first time, keeping them clean takes a little daily effort. But sometimes receipts, paper clutter, and coins just keep coming and coming. Therefore, it is better to spend a little time every day maintaining order in the house than to spend a whole weekend on a general cleaning once a week.

2. Store your media out of sight.

Make a home for CDs, DVDs, video games, and remote controls. They don't need to be in eyesight. You use them less than you think. And if you remove them from your eyesight, maybe you'll use them even less.

3. Keep your work desk minimalistic and clean.

Drawers can adequately house most of the items needed to keep your desk functional. A simple filing system should keep it clear of paper clutter. Then, the next time you sit down to work, you will thank yourself.

4. Process or recycle magazines and newspapers immediately after reading.

If you've finished the paper product, process or recycle it and immediately rid yourself of its clutter.

* Found a good article that your spouse will enjoy? Clip it and recycle the rest.

* Found a good recipe? Put it in your recipe box and recycle the rest.

* An article that your friend will enjoy? Search for it online, send it that way, and then recycle the paper version.

Stacks of magazines and newspapers serve little purpose in our lives but to clutter houses immediately.

5. Get rid of unnecessary decorations.

Grab a box and walk through your living rooms. Then remove decorations from shelves, tables, and walls that aren't absolutely beautiful or meaningful. Believe me: you may like it better than you think (if not, you can always put them back).

6. Fold clean clothes / Remove dirty clothes immediately.

The new way you handle clothes may be the most significant changes you will make in your clutter-free life. I handle each clothes right when I take it off: Clean clothes back to the hanger or drawer and dirty clothes down the clothes chute. That's it. It's really that simple!

7. Always leave room in your coat closet.

There are two main reasons why coats, shoes, and outerwear keep ending up scattered throughout your home rather than in your closet. The first reason is that your coat closet is so full, it's a hassle to put things away and retrieve them quickly. The second reason is maybe you have kids, but that's another story.

8. Remove 3 articles of clothing from your closet just now.

If you are typical, it'll take you roughly 3 minutes to grab 3 articles of clothing that you no longer wear and throw them in a box. As a result, your remaining clothes will fit better in your closet, and your closet will be able to breathe again. You'll feel better about yourself as soon as you do it. Most likely, you'll find yourself inspired to do it again.

9. Unmix and match cups, bowls, plates, and silverware.

Uniformity makes for better storing and accessing. For example, if there is a souvenir mug or bowl that is so important to you, that's perfectly fine. Just don't keep 10 of them.

10. Store kitchen appliances out of sight.

Multicookers, toasters, can openers, coffee makers—they all take up space. And while it may not seem like much space by looking at them, the first time you prepare dinner on a counter without them present, you'll quickly notice the difference when you have a simple, clean kitchen. And if you think it's going to be a hassle putting them away every morning, don't. It takes less than 10 seconds to put each appliance away (once you've found a home for it, that is).

11. Wash dishes right away (or put used dishes in the dishwasher after meals).

Hand washing some dishes takes less time than putting them all in the dishwasher. This applies to cups, breakfast bowls, and silverware. However, if hand washing is just not an option for you, be sure to put used dishes in the dishwasher right away. Nobody likes walking into a kitchen with dishes piled up in the sink or on the counter (and it's even less fun eating in there).

12. Place junk mail immediately into a recycling bin (this also applies to emails).

At first, take note of the natural flow of mail into your home. Placing a recycling container prior to your "mail drop-off zone" can catch most of that junk mail before it even reaches your counter or table. And as a bonus, you'll begin to look through less of it too (think advertisements).

13. Kids' bedroom toys must live in the closet.

Not on the dresser and not on the floor. But in the closet (in boxes, as you already know from previous chapters). And when the closet gets too full of kid's toys, it's time to make some room.

14. Kids have to pick up their toys each evening.

This has countless benefits:

* It teaches kids responsibility.

* It helps kids realize that more isn't always better.

* The home is clean for mom and dad when the kids are in bed.

* It's a clear indication that the day has come to an end, and it's time to rest.

15. Fill your containers for the garbage man.

Use every trash pick-up day as an excuse to fill your recycling containers and garbage cans. Grab a box of old junk from the basement, broken toys from the toy room, old paperwork from the office, old food from the kitchen. But if once a week is too often, do this exercise every other week. You'll get the hang of it and may even begin to enjoy a clutter-free process.

These small steps will help you keep your home clean. As for me, I found the following statement helpful: It is better to spend a little time every day keeping the house tidy than to spend a whole weekend on general cleaning.

◆ ◆ ◆

CHAPTER 28: 25 SIMPLE THINGS TO DO WITH YOUR FAMILY WHILE STUCK AT HOME

As with most of the world, we all spend a lot more time at home in recent days. And it's very important, in these unique times, to redeem the hours and make the most of the moments we have together with our families.

There are negative ramifications to the current state of affairs in our world, but you don't need to see them broadcast in the media. News, good or bad, does not need to overwhelm us.

We can also choose positive effects of free time: Spending time with family, taking longer rests, pursuing new hobbies, and escaping the busyness of our ordinary lives.

With that in mind, here's a list of 25 things to do while stuck at home to redeem the time and make the most of it:

0. Wake up earlier. I need to include this one here because it's essential to start each day with the right attitude. Every day is another opportunity to make the most of it. Don't miss a single chance, even regardless of the circumstances around you.

1. Declutter. Sort your possessions and declutter the stuff in your home. The more we spend time in our home, the more we can recognize what can and should be removed (and the more time we have to do it).

2. Clean up your computer's digital files. This is a whole art! I have devoted several chapters to this process in my previous book:

The 3rd Simple Step to Your Perfect Home: How to Mindfully Clean Your House, Digital, Mind, and Life

3. Make home repairs or a deep clean. If you go through all the steps in the 5 Step book series, that should be more than enough.

4. Read books. You are probably doing this already.

5. Learn a new skill. Been wanting to pick up a new hobby? Now's your chance! Learn a new language, how to cook, or how to code. You can also pick up an instrument or new artistic skill. Because of the Internet, finding a teacher (free or paid) has never been easier.

6. Take a class online. You can easily find plenty of courses for kids and adults available for free online (including Yale's most popular college course ever).

7. Create. I started the *5 Steps* book series as a hobby—somehow, it grew to 5. So start something of your own. Create a blog. Write some stories or poetry. Use your hands in the workshop. Create something you know that we need more than ever.

8. Learn online tools for business. One's thing is for sure— business is going to change very quickly. So learn as quickly as you can how remote work is accomplished and act.

9. Sort through boxes of old photos with kids. Keep the best and put old photos in photo albums or digitize them for future generations. (Prepare for your kids to ask you many questions about your youth along the way.)

10. Have an evening of memories. Sometimes, in order to confidently move into the future, it is necessary to enjoy the past fully. So spend a whole evening looking at your family photos together.

11. Teach your kids life skills. If you haven't already, use the time to teach your kids budgeting, cleaning, laundry, cooking, PC repair, or any other life skills that come to mind.

12. Invent a game. Looking around the room at the supplies you have, make up a new game to play with your kids. Or better yet, invent an entire family competition where each family member gets to pick 1-2 of the events.

13. Dance with your family. I see a lot of those short, choreographed dances being posted on social media. This is super fun for everyone.

14. Learn new board games. Board games can teach us how to think ahead, play out scenarios, and learn from others—all valuable life skills.

15. Evening movie with the family. There's nothing more fun for little kids than staying up past bedtime, eating popcorn, and watching a movie with mom or dad. So make it happen.

16. Watch educational programs. I see a lot of people spending time watching series and television shows, and there's certainly a place for that. But you can also watch educational documentaries about history, science, or events in the world.

17. Make phone calls. Safe to say the phone call is making a comeback again. All those people you would usually see at work, university, or social gatherings—give them a call to say hello.

18. Make video calls. Just click a few buttons on your phone, and suddenly your relative or friend can see you. If you haven't done it before, now's your time.

19. Video chat with friends. Connect and hang out online for a little while with several people at once. It is very funny.

20. Write letters. To a family member or old friend you haven't seen in a while.

21. Go outside. If allowed in your local area, go on long walks or hikes. Spend some time in the park or walk along the river.

22. Workout. We need to be taking care of our physical bodies and taking care of our mental health during this time as well. Look up at-home workouts or yoga and do them together with your family.

23. Have a picnic. If your local community still allows that, you can enjoy time outside as a family (weather-permitting, of course).

24. Organize your recipes and cookbooks (and at the same time, you can cook something new). You can use index cards to keep all your favorites recipes in the same place.

25. Get a pet or plant a houseplant. In this way, you can take care not only of yourself and your family but also share your kindness with other living beings.

There are so many options to make the most of the time now (and probably ahead of us for a little bit longer). Can you add to the list above what you have been doing with your family during this time?

CHAPTER 29: THE POWER OF SIMPLE FRIENDSHIPS

I've been lucky with beautiful friendships in my life. I spend time with people who make me laugh and genuinely care about my family and me. Some of my best friends live close by, but some live far away.

There is an old theory that you become like the people you spend the most time with. For that reason, and because the goodness of others will contribute to your health and happiness, choose simple, positive friendships and spend time with good people.

As for me, I love spending time with people who are:

Wise

Honest

Tolerant

Compassionate

Optimistic

Joyful

Curious

Adventurous

In other words, I like to spend my time with people who embrace life with open hearts and minds. I talk with some of my friends weekly and others less frequently. But they are always close to my heart.

While many of you probably will never meet me, I'm grateful that we get to spend a little time together while you are reading this book. Also, your review, feedback, and kind email messages encourage me to continue writing. I respect you for that.

Today, spend time with people who lift you up and inspire your friends to do good things.

◆ ◆ ◆

CHAPTER 30: HOW TO GET CLUTTERFREE WHEN YOUR FRIENDS ARE NOT

You're giving away the stuff you don't really need. You are always paying off debt. You are becoming more aware of what is important and starting to live life on purpose. What next? Maybe you've realized that one of the essentials is friends. Spending time with people you love is a gift. The only issue is that your friends mustn't change with you (even if you want it).

So how to spend time with the people you love as your new simple self? Maybe your friends haven't changed (and you shouldn't expect them to). But you loved them before, and you can still love them just the way they are. You may have to modify the way you play, but if they love you too, they will likely be open to your recommendations.

Wisely share your new lifestyle, but don't impose it on your friends. Tell them about your plans to get clutterfree, and consume less if you'd like, but don't expect them to embrace the simple life. They would learn from your example, not your arguments. If they need arguments, send them to me.

Consider These Suggestions to Motivate Your Friends:

1. Get Outside.

Instead of meeting for lunch, coffee, or a movie with friends, suggest a walk, hike, or game of tennis. Tell them about your decision to get rid of clutter from your life and what benefits you have received.

2. Community events.

You don't have to be Ukrainian to go to the Ukrainian festival. First, check out what's going on in your city. Chances are there are free decluttering classes and other events to take advantage of. Then, challenge your friends to each suggest an activity and go together.

3. Volunteer together.

Sign up as a group to work at your local charity organization. You can show your friends an example by donating some of your belongings to benefit those who really need them.

Now that you and your friends won't be fighting over different opinions on life, you can really get to know each other and have fun. A new lifestyle may introduce new friends, but it doesn't mean you have to dump your old friends.

◆ ◆ ◆

CHAPTER 31: 10 MONEY QUESTIONS TO ASK YOUR BEST FRIEND

Waste of money contributes to the clutter in our homes, minds, and lives. Clutterfree process isn't just about tidying up our homes. Clutterfree is a holistic approach to life that optimizes our budgets too. But first, some statistics. The statistics concerning our personal use of money are not perfect:

* Less than 1/3 of Americans use a budget.

* Nearly 70% of Americans have less than $1,000 in savings.

* 25% of Americans have no savings at all.

* The average U.S. household owes $7,149 in credit card debt.

* 40% of Americans spend up to half of their income servicing debt.

No wonder money remains the most conflict and a leading cause of stress. The statistics concerning our personal financial habits are sad. And yet, nobody is talking about it (at least not in personal terms).

Money and budget remain some of the least-discussed topics of conversation. It seems we have been conditioned, from a young age, not to talk about it. We fear looking foolish in our decision-making. We worry about stirring up envy or comparison among our family and friends. And most of all, we are concerned about how we will be perceived.

So it seems easier not to talk about it at all. As a result, we often go at it alone, hoping our own judgment will serve us well in our personal financial decisions. However, based on the numbers mentioned above, it is not.

Our silence is ruining our future. Not having this vital conversation is negatively affecting us as persons, as families, and as a society.

Personal finance is a conversation we need to be having with our closest friends. We have so much to learn from one another in all aspects of life—included finances.

While many people do not have financial advisers, almost all of us have friends and relationships with people we look up to. So next time you are with somebody you admire, bring up the topic of personal finance with a spirit of humility. Try asking them some important questions. And the conversation will help you, and probably them, make better financial decisions.

Here are ten money questions to ask your best friend:

1. Do you and your spouse set a financial budget for your home and needs? Do you have good tips on how to find something that really works?

2. Is there a thought process that you use when making large purchases? For example, do you consult with your parents?

3. Can I ask you a money question about what percentage of your income you spend on housing? How did you decide on that particular amount?

4. Do you have a monthly payment on your vehicle? When you bought your car, how did you decide how much you were going to spend?

5. Do you have health insurance? And can I ask how much you pay for it?

6. Did you have to take out a loan for education? Are you doing anything to pay it off early?

7. I have a personal question for you if you don't mind. Are you currently saving some money for retirement? When did you start? And are you happy with how much you are saving?

8. Do you invest any money in the stock market? Where did you go for advice?

9. Could you tell me what is the best piece of financial advice you've ever received?

10. Are you doing anything specific to teach your kids about personal finance? How do they feel about it?

Now, I'm not assuming your friend will have all the perfect answers to these important questions. But the first step to finding the correct answer is simply to ask the right question.

◆ ◆ ◆

CHAPTER 32: 9 HELPFUL STEPS TO STOP OVERSPENDING WITH FRIENDS

According to the statistics, 73% of those who went into debt to keep up with their friends typically keep it a secret. And two-thirds of respondents feel buyer's remorse after spending more than they had planned.

Those are important insights into our spending habits. But, of course, this is not unique to any one society. This is not an American-specific phenomenon. There are actually no differences across the world.

Vitally important to point out, this is also not a socioeconomic phenomenon. People just cannot outearn this temptation.

According to other statistics, 20 percent of households with between $1 million and $10 million in assets in 2004 spent all their income—or more—in a frantic race to keep up with their newfound friends: those with more money than them.

Regardless of generation and net income, the temptation to overspend in an effort to keep up with our friends and their spending habits is common to all of us. I think many of you have felt the same temptation in your own life. But how can we overcome this temptation?

Here are 9 Helpful Steps to Stop Overspending With Friends:

1. Keep in mind the big dreams you have for your life.

Before creating your budget (next step), remember that your budget is not a restrictive device. Just the opposite—your budget is a roadmap to the life you desire: free from debt, focused on your values and most cherished pursuits.

2. Set your own budget.

Or better yet, create a specific spending plan. Be aware of the amount of money you set aside for dining, experiences, and travel per month. And then be vigilant in keeping it.

3. Be honest with your friends.

Surprisingly, some of your friends feel the same way you do. According to the survey, 36% of respondents doubt they can keep up with their friends for another year without going into debt, but nearly 30% don't feel comfortable being the one to say "no" when one of their friends suggests an activity they can't afford. So it's time to break the old trend in your friendship group by being the one to initiate the conversation about the budget.

4. Be clear on your reasoning.

When speaking honestly with your friends, also speak in clear, reasoned terms. Share with them why you decide to spend less:

Is staying out of debt vital to you?

Are you working hard to pay off a student loan?

Maybe generosity is something you want to leave space for in your budget?

Be clear that your reasoning isn't just "I don't have enough money." There is usually a deeper reason and motivation behind it.

5. Look for cheaper alternatives.

Try to look for cheaper alternatives while out with friends. Of course, entirely changing your friend's character or hoping to change your friends' interests is not the only option. So the next time you are out, look for less expensive alternatives:

* Rather than ordering an expensive meal on the menu, order something more reasonably priced.

* Skip the snacks and drinks at your next movie.

* Spend more time in parks and outdoors.

6. Suggest less expensive ideas to your friends.

Good friends try to spend some time together. But that doesn't mean everything they do together needs to cost a lot of money for them. Sometimes it just takes someone to offer up some less expensive, but still good ideas:

An afternoon on the beach.

Frisbee in the park

A hike.

Just be a little creative, and you can find activities for a fun time.

7. Money doesn't affect true friendships.

Some people have a fear that if they don't keep spending the money to be with their friends, they might stop being their friends. Buy that may be the case. Ask yourself: Can you keep overspending and going into debt indefinitely just to be with your friends? Of course not. At some point, something will need to change: either how much money they spend or how much money you spend. Besides, if you need to spend lots of money in order to be with your friends, you probably need new ones.

8. Cut costs in other areas of life.

If spending time with friends and having the financial margin to do so is crucial to you, look for other spending areas in your budget that can be cut:

* Buy less clothing.

* Don't upgrade your PC for new games.

* Pack your lunch for work.

The clutter-free method is the intentional promotion of the things we most value by removing anything that distracts us from it. If applying a clutter-free approach in one area frees up more money to be spent with your friends, then that's exactly the point of it.

9. There will be other opportunities.

One thing I know to be true of life—it goes on. Opportunities come, and opportunities go. And sometimes bypassing an opportunity today means you can enjoy a different one tomorrow—when you are in a better stage of life financially. Taking a step back from overspending to keep up with your friends doesn't mean you'll never be able to spend money with friends again. Just the opposite! It'll help put you in a more financially stable place so that you can do even more of it in the future.

Having good friends doesn't mean you have to go broke. You can have both good friends and enough money. It just might take some intentional decisions to find the right balance.

◆ ◆ ◆

CHAPTER 33: 101 CLUTTER-FREE GIFT IDEAS

T he numbers are a retailer's dream but a consumer's nightmare. According to statistics, the average American spends around $1,250 during the holiday season on gifts, travel, and entertainment.

These numbers might be acceptable if the gifts we were buying and the possessions we were accumulating will actually increase the happiness in our lives. But commonly, that's not the case.

Over half of us will receive unwanted gifts every year! And eighteen percent of gifts are never used by the person who receives them, and 4 percent are immediately thrown into the trash!

The reality is that our homes are already overcrowded with unuseful stuff. Do you want to add more layers of stuff on top of it?

So what then can we give that won't add to the clutter problem? There are 101 clutter-free gift ideas:

Time

1. Parent/Child Date

2. Family Portrait Session

3. Prepped Meals

4. Personal Chef

5. Babysitter

6. Pet Sitting

7. House Cleaner

8. Car Wash

9. Gas Card

10. Oil Change

11. Shoveling

12. Sunday Brunch

13. Yard Service

14. Date Night Out

15. Professional Organizer

Experiences

16. Family Vacation

17. Community Theater

18. Concert Tickets

19. Comedy Club

20. Bowling Tickets

21. Carriage Ride

22. City Tour

23. Dinner Gift Card

24. Charitable Donation

25. Escape Room

26. Facial

27. Horseback Riding

28. Indoor Rock Climbing

29. Laser Tag

30. Mini-Golf

31. Movie Pass

32. Orchestra

33. Overnight Camp

34. Round of Golf

35. Shooting Range

36. Ski Lift

37. Spa Day

38. Sporting Event

39. Theater Tickets

40. Trampoline Park

41. Travel Voucher

42. Water Park

43. Zoo / Aquarium

44. Manicure (Pedicure)

45. Massage

Classes

46. Cooking

47. Baking

48. Cake Decorating

49. Coding

50. Dance

51. Foreign Language

52. Home Brewing

53. Improv

54. Karate

55. Magic

56. Master Class

57. Music

58. Painting/Art

59. Photography

60. Private Coach

61. Scuba Diving

62. Sports

63. Swimming

64. Tennis

65. Voice

66. Yoga

Memberships

67. Amazon Prime

68. Audible

69. Disney+

70. Netflix

71. Art Museum

72. Science Museum

73. Children's Museum

74. AAA

75. Community Pool

76. Dollar Shave Club

77. Farm Share
78. Hello Fresh
79. National Parks
80. Simplify Magazine
81. State Parks
82. Theme Park
83. Toy Library
84. YMCA

Consumables
85. Snack Box
86. Local Foods
87. Baked Goods
88. Chocolates
89. Coffee Beans
90. Coffee Gift Card
91. Desserts
92. Fruit Basket
93. Meat
94. Cheese
95. Olive Oil
96. Tacos
97. Tea
98. Wine
99. Video Game Gift Card
100. Flowers

My favorite category, which deserves special mention

101. Books

* If you like this book, then, no doubt, you will like my other books as well:

5 STEPS

The 1st Simple Step to Your Perfect Home: How to Methodologically Sort Through All Items, Keep Important, and Get Rid of Unnecessary

The 2nd Simple Step to Your Perfect Home: How to Methodically Put All Necessary Items in the Optimal Places and Organize Everyday Life

The 3rd Simple Step to Your Perfect Home: How to Mindfully Clean Your House, Digital, Mind, and Life

MINDFUL MOMENTS COLLECTION

The Mindful Thrift: How to Appreciate What We Have and Save What We Do Not Notice

The Mindful Nutrition: How to Enjoy the True Taste of Food, Have a Slim Body and 33 (+3) Home Cooking Recipes for a Delicious Degustation

The Mindful Eating for Beginners: Step-by-Step Guide for Lifelong Health and Collection of Quick & Easy Recipes for Every Day

BIG LITTLE STORIES

Escape to Myself

Sea Soul

The Mountain of Desires

An Epidemic 1,000 Years Before Us

You can easily add to this gift list any options at your discretion. The main thing is to understand the essence: The best gift is the one that can give pleasant emotions or solve a problem.

◆ ◆ ◆

CHAPTER 34: 9 THINGS YOU SHOULD NEVER MINIMIZE

U sing the 5 Steps Method, we strive for less stuff to experience more life. We learn how to detach from our possessions, limit technology, manage our finances with more intention, and organize schedules.

Our schedules must get pared down to the most important appointments. Instead of chasing material things, we have to open calendars for family time, meeting a friend for lunch, reading, and pursuing a passion. Simplicity must become our lifestyle. We have to learn to ask ourselves important question before adding any item to our life:

"How can this make my life easier?"

Simplicity takes more intention than buying things, so we learn to value the weight of every decision. And the value of an item or experience becomes more than a price tag. The 5 Step approach is a journey of heart and soul.

This matter of the heart requires that we take great care to cut the non-essentials and cultivate the things we should never minimize. It's how we can maximize the benefits of a clutter-free life.

But in the life of each of us, there are things that we should not get rid of. **And I want to tell you about nine things you should never**

minimize:

1. Dreams

Our passions and dreams often end up on the chopping block when we are overwhelmed with crammed calendars and schedules. Yet, simplicity should never stifle the life-giving joys in our life. When we release our attachment to stuff and busyness, we have more space, time, and energy to pursue and participate in our passions. If we ever feel the need to minimize the very thing that makes us come alive, we've lost sight of who we truly are. Simple life creates space for the development of our dreams and passions, and we then realize the burden our stuff has over us.

2. Appreciation

I believe that the most significant expression of appreciation is simplicity. When a person is truly grateful for what matters most, no amount of possessions could change that contentment. On the other hand, a room full of gadgets, toys, and forgotten impulse purchases steals our gratitude by complicating our lives. To live a life of gratitude, we recognize that the essentials are enough, and we can experience how they enhance our existence. Appreciation isn't just being thankful for what you have. It's believing that you have is enough for the perfect life.

3. Generosity

Decluttering is not an excuse to not be generous. On the contrary, it is the most excellent excuse to be more generous. Ridding our lives of excess offers the apparent opportunity to donate our possessions that can be useful to someone. But there are other not-so-obvious reasons we should never minimize generosity: we create more space to offer our space, time, meals, service, and gifts to others. Our unburdened schedules allow more investments in relationships, more hobbies, and more financial resources. Our minds are free of clutter, so we can create more and share more of our talents. Have less, give more.

4. Empathy

We don't like to admit it, but when we have a strong belief about the way we live, sometimes we minimize our empathy for those who live something differently. Becoming simple is never a destination. It's a journey of reducing the outside influencers. But non-simple people are not outsiders. They are people like you and me. They are faithful leaders, inspiring mentors, guides, and peacemakers. The way we treat others who struggle with the burden of things will either maximize their value to us or minimize our value to them. Choose carefully and wisely.

5. Relationships

We should never commit so intently to this clutter-free way of life that we alienate our family, faithful friends, or the potential new positive relationships. There may be a time when decluttering harmful or unhealthy relationships is appropriate. However, decluttering isn't about living a reclusive. Instead, we minimize to un-clutter our lives from that which robs our focus, time, and energy from investing in the most important people in our lives.

6. Community

Decluttering should never mean less community. In fact, a clutter-free life opens our lives to more community and the opportunity to live alongside others. Our society, those outside our immediate family but who share in our activities around the home, school, work, or neighborhood, should benefit from our clutter-free life. The amount of time we gain, the items that can be reused or repurposed by someone in need, and the space we offer in less crowded lives are practical ways to live in the community intentionally.

7. Forgiveness

If you've ever been in any kind of relationship that has lasted more than a few weeks, you know that forgiveness is part of life. If we minimize our capacity to forgive people (and ourselves), we can never hope to grow or change. Minimizing the value of forgiveness will reduce our capacity for genuine connection. A significant relationship demands forgiveness.

8. Education

Education in any form, when applied, enriches our lives to greater understanding and action. To minimize our education is to reduce our potential to change the world. For any educational investment, we gain, at the very least, a deepened capacity to think and to relate to the world around us.

9. Joy

Our inaccurate source of value often causes the absence of joy. It is a fundamental paradox: The more we buy, the less happy we are. It may seem boring to live a life with less stuff, but that's only because we haven't freed ourselves from the chains of believing our value comes from what we own. Less stuff is more joy because, in this case, we have only what we really appreciate. To free ourselves from comparisons and the joy-reducing value system, the answer lies in the freedom of clutter-free life.

By freeing yourself from unnecessary things, you are freeing your life. But how to distinguish unnecessary trash from values in life? The answer is simple: listen to your heart. No one can tell you what is good and bad for you. You live your life, so it's up to you to decide.

◆ ◆ ◆

CHAPTER 35: SIMPLE JOURNALING AND WHY YOU SHOULD KEEP ONE

One of the best ways to process your journey toward a simple life is journaling! Journals help you better connect with your values, goals, and emotions. They also help keep track of personal development.

The reality is this: life happens fast—sometimes too fast—and we seldom take the time to stop and look at what's happening around us. But by keeping a journal, we leave a footprint for us to remember how each moment made us feel. So it's time to keep simple journaling.

There are plenty of reasons for simple journaling, but here are five concrete things I think are worthwhile writing about:

1. The magic of free space.

I am a firm believer in this: free space is where the magic happens. I've shared this idea many times, both in this book as well as in all previous. The free, quiet time we give ourselves is the perfect chance to slow down and recharge. And when we slow down, we allow ourselves to learn, be grateful, and live with intention.

2. Write about gratitude.

Focusing on the things we are thankful for is a great way to remove ourselves from unconsciousness. Of course, sometimes we place importance on what we already have, but we probably don't do it as often as we should. Going through the process of writing down these things should result in greater realization, which means we have a better chance of remembering how happy we are.

3. Remember the little things.

I think far too many times we try to place emphasis on the "bigger" things in life. And we end up forgetting how important all of the little things are. But writing them down in a journal is a surefire way never to forget.

4. Realize your experience.

Your journey towards a simple life is your own experience. It's about crafting a way of living that you want to experience. It's about designing a life that's right for you best. Your journal is a place to share with yourself the reasons why you deserve a life filled with happiness. It's a place to remind yourself of this one very important thing—you have everything you need to be happy.

5. Document your path.

Our lives are unique. We only have one try at making the most of it, and we should want to do just that. We should spend our time and energy on experiences that we'll remember, rather than on things we'll give away. And these are among the things we should remember to write about.

Simple journaling will help you let go of distractions and fears. Simple journaling will help you figure out what's most important in your way, at home, and at work. Simple journaling will help you turn down the noise that disrupts the quiet of your heart and soul.

Final Words

I want to take this opportunity to thank you from the bottom of my heart for choosing to read my work. I am humbled by your decision to devote your time and effort to this endeavor, and it is an honor and a privilege to have the chance to share my ideas with you.

As a writer, I am aware of how crucial it is to establish a significant and lasting connection with readers. It is my sincere wish that this book has touched you in some manner and that you have appreciated the knowledge and advice I have provided.

I have had the honor of working with countless people who have overcome incredible obstacles to accomplish their objectives throughout my employment. I have been moved by the tenacity and resolve of those who are dedicated to living their best lives, whether they be athletes, company leaders, or regular people like you.

In order to craft a message that is both relatable and actionable, I relied on both my own experiences and the experiences of others when I was writing this book. I wanted to offer you a tool that would both inspire you and equip you with the methods and tactics you need to succeed.

I think the advice and techniques in this book can help you accomplish your objectives, whether you want to strengthen your relationships, be happier, or pursue your dreams. I have consulted a variety of resources to develop a message that is both useful and inspirational, ranging from the most recent scientific findings to the knowledge of ancient philosophers.

However, this book has been more than anything else a labor of affection. I firmly believe that each and every one of us has the potential to lead meaningful lives, and it is my sincere wish that this work has assisted you in realizing your own potential.

As I think back on this experience, I'm incredibly appreciative of all the people who have helped me along the path. My incredible team of collaborators—from my family and friends to my editors and publishers—have helped me to realize this endeavor.

Most significantly, I want to thank you, the reader, for reading. Your choice to read this book has motivated me to carry on spreading my message, and I'm appreciative for the chance to have impacted your life.

I trust this book has surpassed your expectations and given you the motivation and resources you need to accomplish your objectives. May you prosper and develop as you go along and never forget that anything is attainable if you put your mind to it.

Once again, I want to thank you for reading my work and for your support. I hope that this book has made a lasting impact on you because it has been an incredible honor for me to share my thoughts and ideas with you.

With the utmost respect and gratitude,

Ashley Cortez

Printed in Great Britain
by Amazon

39877456R00084